PSYCHO-ANALYSIS AND THE WAR NEUROSES

PSYCHO-ANALYSIS AND THE WAR NEUROSES

SÁNDOR FERENCZI,
KARL ABRAHAM,
ERNEST JONES,
ERNST SIMMEL,
SIGMUND FREUD

ISBN: 978-93-5614-367-8

Published: 1921

LECTOR HOUSE LLP
E-MAIL: lectorpublishing@gmail.com

THE INTERNATIONAL PSYCHO-ANALYTICAL LIBRARY
NO. 2

PSYCHO-ANALYSIS AND THE WAR NEUROSES

BY

**DRS. S. FERENCZI (BUDAPEST),
KARL ABRAHAM (BERLIN),
ERNST SIMMEL (BERLIN),
AND
ERNEST JONES (LONDON)**

INTRODUCTION BY
PROF. SIGM. FREUD (VIENNA)

EDITED BY
ERNEST JONES

1921

CONTENTS

Page

I.

INTRODUCTION BY
PROFESSOR SIGM. FREUD, VIENNA.

This little book on the War Neuroses, with which the Verlag opens the "Internationale psychoanalytische Bibliothek", deals with a subject which until lately engaged the greatest current interest. When the subject came up for discussion at the Fifth Psycho-Analytical Congress at Budapest (September, 1918), official representatives of the Central European Powers were present to obtain information from the lectures and discussions. The hopeful result of this first meeting was the promise that psycho-analytical institutions should be established, where medical men qualified in analysis might find the means and time to study the nature of these puzzling illnesses and the therapeutic value of psycho-analysis in them. However, before these results could be achieved the war came to an end, the government organisations broke down, and interest in war neuroses gave place to other concerns. At the same time, significantly enough, most of the neurotic diseases which had been brought about by the war disappeared on the cessation of the war conditions. The opportunity, therefore, for a thorough investigation of these affections was unfortunately missed. However, one must add, it is to be hoped that it will be a very long time before such an opportunity again occurs. This episode, now a thing of the past, has not been without importance for the spread of the knowledge of psycho-analysis. Many medical men, who had previously held themselves aloof from psycho-analysis, have been brought into close touch with its theories through their service with the army compelling them to deal with the question of the war neuroses. The reader can easily gather from Ferenczi's contribution to the subject with what hesitation and misgivings this advance was made. Some of the factors, such as the psycho-genetic origin of the symptoms, the significance of unconscious impulses, and the part that the primary advantage of being ill plays in the adjusting psychical conflicts ("flight into disease"), all of which had long before been discovered and described as operating in the neuroses of peace time, were found also in the war neuroses and almost generally accepted. The work of E. Simmel has shown what results may be obtained if the war neurotic is treated by the cathartic method, which, as is well known, was the first stage of the psycho-analytic technique.

From the advance thus made towards psycho-analysis, however, one need not assume that the opposition to it has been reconciled or neutralised. One might think that when a man, who had hitherto not accepted any of a number of connected conclusions, suddenly finds himself in the position of being convinced of the truth of a part of them, he would weaken in his opposition and adopt an attitude of respectful attention, lest the other part, of which he has no personal experience, and therefore upon which he is unable to form a personal opinion, should also prove to be correct.

This other part of the psycho-analytical theory which is not touched upon in the study of the war neuroses is that the driving forces which find expression in the formation of symptoms are sexual in nature, and that the neurosis is the result of the conflict between the ego and the sexual impulses which it has repudiated. The term "sexuality" is to be taken here in the broader sense customary in psycho-analysis, and not to be confused with the narrower sense of "genitality". Now it is quite correct, as Ernest Jones points out in his contribution, that this part of the theory has not hitherto been demonstrated in relation to the war neuroses. The work which could prove this part has not yet been carried out. It may be that the war neuroses are unsuitable material for this proof. However, the opponents of psycho-analysis, whose repugnance to sexuality has shown itself to be stronger than their logic, have hastened to proclaim that investigation of the war neuroses has finally disproved this part of the psycho-analytical theory. In this pronouncement they have been guilty of a slight confusion. If the—up to the present superficial—investigation of war neuroses has not shown that the sexual theory of the neuroses is correct, that is quite another matter from showing that this theory is incorrect.

With an impartial attitude and some willingness it should not be difficult to find the way to further elucidation.

The war neuroses, in so far as they differ from the ordinary neuroses of peace time through particular peculiarities, are to be regarded as traumatic neuroses, whose existence has been rendered possible or promoted through an ego-conflict. In Abraham's contribution there are plain indications of this ego-conflict; the English and American authors whom Jones quotes have also recognised it. The conflict takes place between the old ego of peace time and the new war-ego of the soldier, and it becomes acute as soon as the peace-ego is faced with the danger of being killed through the risky undertakings of his newly formed parasitical double. Or one might put it, the old ego protects itself from the danger to life by flight into the traumatic neurosis in defending itself against the new ego which it recognises as threatening its life. The National Army was therefore the condition, and fruitful soil, for the appearance of war neuroses; they could not occur in professional soldiers, or mercenaries.

The other feature of the war neurosis is that it is a traumatic neurosis, such as is well known to occur in peace time after fright or severe accidents, without any reference to an ego-conflict.

The theory of the sexual aetiology of the neuroses, or as we prefer to call it, the sexual hunger (libido) theory, was originally put forward only as regards the transference neuroses of peace conditions, and can be easily demonstrated in them by using the analytic technique. But its application to those other affections, which more recently we have grouped together as the narcissistic neuroses, meets with difficulties. Ordinary cases of Dementia praecox, Paranoia and Melancholia are fundamentally very unsuitable material for the proof of the sexual hunger (libido) theory and for reaching an understanding of it, for which reason psychiatrists, who neglect the transference neuroses cannot be reconciled to it. The traumatic neuroses (of peace time) have always been reckoned to be the most refractory in this respect, so that the appearance of the war neuroses does not add any fresh factor to the former situation.

Only by advancing and making use of the idea of a "narcissistic sexual hunger (libido)", that is to say, a mass of sexual energy that attaches itself to the ego and satisfies itself with this as otherwise it does only with an object, has it been possible to extend the sexual hunger (libido) theory to the narcissistic neuroses, and this entirely legitimate development of the concept of sexuality bids fair to do for these severer neuroses and for the psychoses all that one can expect from an empirically and tentatively progressing theory. The traumatic neurosis of peace time will also fit into this group when researches into the correlation undoubtedly subsisting between shock, anxiety, and narcissistic sexual hunger (libido) have reached success.

If the traumatic and war neuroses emphasise the influence of the danger to life and not at all, or not clearly enough, that of the "denial of love", on the other hand the aetiological claim of the former factor appearing there so powerfully, is lacking in the usual transference neuroses of peace time. Indeed it is vulgarly supposed that these latter sufferings are only promoted by indulgence, high-living and ease, which provide an interesting contrast to the conditions of life under which the war neuroses break out. If psycho-analysts, who find their patients have become ill through the "denial of love", through the ungratified demands of the sexual hunger (libido), were to follow the example of their opponents, they would maintain that either there are no danger neuroses, or that the affections following on terror are not neuroses. This has naturally never crossed their minds. On the contrary, they see the convenient possibility of combining in one conception the two apparently divergent sets of facts. In the traumatic and war neuroses the ego of the individual protects itself from a danger that either threatens it from without, or is embodied in a form of the ego itself, in the transference neuroses of peace time the ego regards its own sexual hunger (libido) as a foe, the demands of which appear threatening to it. In both cases the ego fears an injury; in the one case through the sexual hunger (libido) and in the other from outside forces. One might even say that in the case of the war neuroses the thing feared, is after all an inner foe, in distinction from the pure traumatic neuroses and approximating to the transference neuroses. The theoretical difficulties which stand in the way of such a unifying conception do not appear to be insurmountable; one can with full right designate the repression which underlies every neurosis, as a reaction to a trauma, as an elementary traumatic neurosis.

Spring 1919.

II.

SYMPOSIUM HELD AT THE FIFTH INTERNATIONAL PSYCHO-ANALYTICAL CONGRESS AT BUDAPEST, SEPTEMBER 1918:

1. Dr. S. Ferenczi, Budapest.

Ladies and Gentlemen,

With your permission I will commence my exposition of the very serious and important subject that is the theme of my lecture to-day with the recital of a little story which will lead us straightway into the revolutionising events of this war. A Hungarian, who had the opportunity of observing at close quarters a part of the revolutionary upheaval in Russia, told me that the new revolutionary rulers of a Russian town found with consternation that the change from the old to the new regime had not taken place as rapidly as it should have done according to their doctrinal calculations. According to the teachings of the materialistic idea of history they could have set up the new social order immediately after they had got the entire power into their hands. Instead of this, irresponsible elements, which were antagonistic to any new order of things, obtained the upper hand, so that the power gradually slipped from the hands of the originators of the revolution. Then the leaders of the movement put their heads together in order to find out what had gone wrong in their calculations. Finally they agreed that perhaps the materialistic idea was after all too one-sided, as it only took into consideration the economic and commercial relations, and had forgotten to take into account one small matter, the feelings and thoughts of man, in a word, the psyche. They were sufficiently consistent to send emissaries immediately to German speaking countries, in order to obtain psychological works, so that they might get at least subsequently some knowledge of this neglected science. Many thousands of human lives fell victims, perhaps to no purpose, to this omission of the revolutionaries; the failure of their efforts resulted in their making one discovery however, namely, that of the mind.

A somewhat similar thing has occurred among neurologists during the war. The war has produced an enormous number of nervous disorders which call for elucidation and cure; however, the familiar organic-mechanistic explanation hitherto adopted—which in some way corresponds to the materialistic idea of history in sociology—completely failed. The mass-experiment of the war has produced various severe neuroses, including those in which there could be no question of a mechanical influence, and the neurologists have likewise been forced to recognise that something was missing in their calculations, and this something was again—the psyche.

To some extent we can forgive sociology for this omission; indeed the estimation of mental elements in the science of society has hitherto been in fact a very trifling one. However, we cannot spare neurologists the reproach of having so long disregarded the pioneer researches of Breuer and Freud concerning the psychical determination of many nervous disturbances, and of having required the terrible experiences of the war to set them right in this respect. And yet a science—psycho-analysis—has existed for more than twenty years to which many investigators had devoted the whole of their efforts, and which had helped us to unexpected and important knowledge of the mechanisms of mental life and its disturbances.

In my lecture today I shall confine myself to demonstrating the introduction of psycho-analysis into modern neurology, an introduction which has been effected to some small extent openly, but for the most part with hesitation and under false colours, and I will briefly communicate the theoretical principles upon which rest the psycho-analytical conceptions of the "traumatic neuroses" which have been observed during the war[1].

Soon after the outbreak of the war there flamed up again the great controversy, which had been carried on for more than ten years, concerning the nature of the traumatic neuroses which Oppenheim had in his time placed in a class by themselves. Oppenheim hastened to make use of the experiences of the war, which exposed so many thousands of men to sudden shocks, as supporting his old views, according to which the phenomena of these neuroses always came about, as the result of physical alterations in the nervous centres, (or in the peripheral nerves which secondarily affect those of the centre). The nature of the shock itself and its influence upon the method of functioning he described in very general, one might even say, phantastic terms. Links were "cut out" from the chain of the innervation mechanism, most delicate elements "displaced", paths "blocked", connections torn asunder, obstacles to conduction created, etc. With these and similar comparisons, from which, however, all basis in fact was tacking, Oppenheim sketched an impressive picture of the material correlation of the traumatic neuroses.

The alterations in structure which would take place in the brain through the trauma Oppenheim conceived as a delicate physical process similar to that which occurs in the iron filing when it comes into contact with the magnet.

The sarcastic Gaupp designates such specious physical and physiological speculations as brain mythology and molecular mythology. But in our opinion he does mythology an injustice.

The material brought forward by Oppenheim to support his views was in no way suited to uphold his abstruse theories. To be sure, he described with his usual precision characteristic symptoms, which this war has produced in deplorable

[1] I shall only here take into consideration the most important publications out of the enormous amount of neurological literature of the war, and only in so far as this refers to psycho-analysis. I am indebted to Dr. M. Eitingon and Prof. Dr. A. v. Sarbó for access to the necessary authorities.

numbers, and also gave to them somewhat high-sounding names (Akinesia am-nestica, Myotonoklonia trepidans) that said nothing as to their nature; these de-scriptions, however, are not especially convincing with reference to his theoretical conceptions[2].

There were, it is true, many who agreed with Oppenheim's views, though for the most part with limitations. Goldscheider holds that the cause of these nervous symptoms is partly physical and partly psychical; Cassierer, Schuster and Birn-baum are of the same opinion. Wollenberg's question, as to whether the war neu-roses were caused through emotion or shock, Aschaffenburg answered by stating that there was here concerned the joint effect of emotion and concussion. As one of the few who obstinately persisted in maintaining the mechanistic idea I will mention Lilienstein, who categorically demanded that the word and the concept of "mind", also that of "functional" and "psychic", and more especially that of "psycho-genesis" should be struck out of the medical terminology; he maintained that this would simplify the conflict and facilitate the investigation, treatment and examination of the casualties; the progressive anatomical technique would cer-tainly sooner or later discover the material foundations of the neuroses.

We must here refer to the train of thought pursued by V. Sarbó, who seeks for the cause of the war neuroses in the microscopical destruction of tissue and hemor-rhages in the central organ of the nervous system; these, he says, originate through direct concussion, sudden pressure of the cerebro-spinal fluid, compression of the spinal cord in the foramen magnum, etc. V. Sarbó's theory is only supported by a few authors. In this connection I might mention Sachs and Freud, who consider that the shock puts the nerve cells into a condition of heightened excitability and exhaustability, which is then the immediate cause of the neuroses. Finally, Bauer and Fauser look upon the traumatic neuroses as the nervous results of disturbanc-es of the endocrine glands produced by the shock, and as similar therefore to the post-traumatic Basedow's disease.

Strümpell was one of the first to oppose the purely organic-mechanistic idea of the war neuroses. He had, moreover, for some time previously referred to certain psychical factors in the causation of the traumatic neuroses. He made the accurate observation that in railway accidents, etc., those who suffered from a severe neuro-sis were for the most part those who had an *interest* in being able to prove an injury as caused by the trauma: for example, persons who were insured against accidents and wished to obtain a large sum of money, or those who instituted proceedings against the railway company for compensation for injury. Similar or much more severe shocks have, however, no lasting nervous results if the accident happens during sport through one's own carelessness, especially under circumstances that exclude the hope of compensation for injury as those mentioned, so that the pa-tient has no interest in remaining ill, but every interest in the speediest recovery. Strümpell asserts that the shock neuroses always develop secondarily and purely psycho-genetically as the result of desire of gain; he gave medical men the well-

---

[2] One of Oppenheim's critics has suggested that these words so difficult to pronounce might be used as test words in the examination of paralytic disturbances of speech, so that they might at least be of some good.

meant advice not to take seriously the complaints of these patients, like Oppenheim, but to bring them back as soon as possible to life and work through the smallest allowance or through withdrawal of their pension. The representations of Strümpell created a great impression in the medical world even in peace time; they led to the idea of the "compensation hysteria"; the sufferers, however, were treated not much better than if they were malingerers. Strümpell now suggests that the war neuroses are also neuroses of covetousness, which serve the patients' purpose in getting free from the military authorities with the highest possible pension. Accordingly he demands a strict examination and expert opinion of the neuroses occurring in military persons. The content of the pathogenic ideas is always a wish — the wish for material compensation, for remaining far from infections and danger — and this wish acts along auto-suggestive paths in fixing more firmly the symptoms, the persistence of morbid sensations and of innervation disturbances of motility.

Much of the foregoing train of thought of Strümpell sounds to the analyst very probable. For he knows from his analytical experience that neurotic symptoms in general represent wish fulfilments, and also the fixation of unpleasant mental impressions and their pathogenic state is familiar to him. Still he has to reproach the one-sidedness of Strümpell's train of thought: for instance, in the undue prominence of the cognitive aspect of the pathogenic experience and the neglect of its affective side, as well as the complete ignoring of the unconscious psychical processes, with which already Kurt Singer, Schuster and Gaupp had reproached him. Strümpell also has a presentiment that these neurotic forms of illness can only be explained by means of a psychical investigation; he does not, however, tell us his method of work with reference to this. Probably he understands by psychical exploration simply a careful questioning of the patient as to his material circumstances and concerning his motives for seeking a pension. We must on the other hand protect ourselves in that he calls this exploration "a method of individual psycho-analysis". There is only one procedure that has a right to this name, that which the strict method of psycho-analysis has made its own.

As an argument in favour of the psycho-genesis of the war neuroses it is a remarkable fact, which has been pointed out by Mörchen, Bonhöffer and others, that the traumatic neuroses are practically never seen in prisoners of war. The prisoners of war have no interest in remaining sick after being captured, and they cannot reckon on compensation, pension and sympathy from their surroundings while they are away from home. They feel themselves in their captivity secure for the time being from the dangers of the war. The theory of the mechanistic shock can never explain to us this difference in the behaviour of our own soldiers and prisoners of war.

Evidence as regards the psycho-genesis rapidly accumulated. Schuster and many other observers refer to the disproportion between the trauma and its results on the nervous system. Severe neuroses arise from minimal shocks, while it is just the severe wounds accompanied by great shock that for the most part are not followed by nervous disturbances. Kurt Singer lays still greater stress on the disproportion between trauma and neurosis, and even endeavours to explain this fact psychologically: "In the kind of psychic trauma that comes on in a flash, in the terror, in the paralysing horror, we are concerned with cases of difficulty or impossibility of adaptation to the stimulus". In a severe wound there is a discharge of the suddenly increased tension without anything further; when, however, no severe external injury exists the excessive affect is discharged "by means of a sudden abreaction through physical phenomena". As the Freudian expression "abreaction" shows, psycho-analysis must have been in the mind of the writer when he thought out this theory. The expression sounds like a delayed response to the Breuer-Freudian conversion theory. However, it soon appears that Singer represents this process far too rationalistically; he looks upon the symptoms of the traumatic neuroses as the result of an effort on the part of the patient to find a comprehensible explanation of the (to him) inexplicable morbid process. Thus the work of this author is still far removed from the dynamic conception of the psychical processes of which psycho-analysis has taught us.

Hauptmann, Schmidt and others drew attention to the relation in time in the development of the symptoms in the war neuroses. If it is a question of a mechanical injury then the effect should be strongest immediately after the operation of the force. Instead of which one finds that the men thrown into a state of shock still make purposive endeavours to arrange for their safety the moment after the trauma, such as to get to the dressing station, etc., and only after having put themselves under safe conditions do they collapse and the symptoms develop. In some cases the symptoms appear only when the men have to return to the firing line after a period of rest. Schmidt is quite right when he refers this conduct of the patients to the psychical factors; he suggests that the neurotic symptoms develop only after the state of a transitory disturbance of consciousness has disappeared and the men who have suffered the shock re-experience in memory the dangerous situation. We would say: These injured men behave like the mother who rescues her child from a danger which threatens its life with calm imperturbability and disregard of death, but faints after the act has been accomplished. It is immaterial as regards the judgment of the psychological situation that here the person saved was not a beloved stranger, but the beloved person himself.

I place Nonne in the forefront of those authors who have laid particular stress on the psycho-genesis of the traumatic neuroses of the war. Not only because he recognised that the symptoms of the war shock neuroses were without exception hysterical, but because he was also able to cause the severest war neurotic symptoms to disappear for a time or to recall them by hypnotic and suggestive measures. This excluded the possibility even of a "molecular" disturbance in the nerve tissues; a disturbance that can be set right by means of psychic influences can itself have been nothing else than psychical.

This therapeutic argument had the greatest effect; by degrees a marked silence fell over the mechanistic school, and attempts were frequently made to explain their former utterances psycho-genetically. The quarrel from now onwards lay entirely between the supporters of the various psychological theories.

How is one to explain the method of working of psychical factors, and also the fact of the psychogenic condition being more severe than the impressive forms of disorders of organic origin?

One is reminded of the old theory of Charcot, that terror and the memory of it can produce in a similar manner physical symptoms after the nature of hypnosis and auto-hypnosis, just as they are intentionally brought about by the post-hypnotic command of the hypnotist.

This reverting to Charcot means nothing less than paving the way to fruitless speculations and the re-discovery of the sources from which finally psycho-analysis sprang; for we know that the first researches of Breuer and Freud into the psychical mechanisms of hysterical phenomena originated directly from the influence of Charcot's clinical and experimental experiences. Hysterics suffer from reminiscences: this, the primary axiom of the germinating psycho-analysis, is really the continuation, deepening, and generalisation of the ideas of Charcot applied to the neuroses of shock; the idea of the lasting effect of a sudden affect and of the association of certain expressions of affect with the memory of the thing experienced is common to both.

Let us now compare with this the views of German neurologists on the genesis of the war neuroses. Goldscheider says: "Sudden and terrifying impressions can leave behind affects direct and also with the associative help of ideation; to these memory pictures are due the results of increased and lowered excitability. Thus it is the emotion, the terror, which bestows upon the trauma the distribution and fixation of the nervous results of the stimulus, which never occurs with the purely physical stimulus itself". It is easy to recognise that this description is borrowed from the traumatic theory of Charcot and the Freudian conversion theory.

Gaupp's opinion is similar: "In spite of all the methods of modern experimental psychology and of all the more precise and more delicate methods of technique for neurological and psychiatric investigation, there remains a residue, and not an insignificant one, in which we do not arrive at a diagnosis by means of the present exact neurological and psychiatric investigation of the condition at the moment present, but only through its connection with an exact anamnesis and with a laborious exploration of the pathogenesis of the existing condition". Gaupp accepts even explicitly a Freudian postulation, in that he describes the war neuroses as a flight from psychic conflicts into illness and, alluding to psycho-analysis, he says: "Much preferable is the postulate of the effects of the unconscious on consciousness and the physical system than a psychological theory which seeks by words taken from the sciences of anatomy and physiology to gloss over the fact that the path from the physical to the mental and vice versa is entirely unknown to us". In another place he goes still further and puts the psycho-analytical postulate of the unconscious in the centre of the whole problem. "If one only admits that mental processes can react upon the body even when they do not lie in the conscious field of vision, then most of the supposed difficulties disappear". In this connection Hauptmann must also be mentioned. He looks upon the traumatic neuroses as mental illnesses psycho-genetically elaborated and caused through emotional factors, and their symptoms as "unconscious further elaboration of the emotional factors along paths of least resistance".

Bonhoeffer seems to have completely accepted the psychologically complex experiences of psycho-analysis. He holds that the traumatic symptoms are "psycho-neurotic fixations, dissociation phenomena which have been rendered possible through the resultant splitting off of the affect from its ideational content under the influence of the violent emotion".

Birnbaum showed in his excellent summary of the literature of the traumatic neuroses that in many of the explanations of these neuroses (for example, in Strümpell's theory of covetousness) is summed up a psychogenic wish of hysteria, and says: "If the psychogenic wish, the wish fixation, etc. is an essential component of hysteria then it belongs unconditionally in the definition of the disorder". Psycho-analysis has long maintained this; as is well known, it regards the neurotic symptoms as expressions of unconscious wishes or as reactions to them.

Vogt also refers to the "famous Freudian statement" according to which the troubled mind flies into illness and he acknowledges that "the compulsion which originates from this is more often unconscious than conscious". Liepmann divides the symptoms of the traumatic neuroses into the direct results of the psychic trauma and into "finally adjusted psychic mechanisms". Schuster speaks of symptoms which are evoked by means of "unconscious processes".

You see, therefore, ladies and gentlemen, that the experiences among war neurotics gradually led further than to the discovery of the mind; they led neurologists very nearly to the discovery of psycho-analysis. When we read in the more recent literature on the subject, of the ideas and views which have become so familiar,—abreaction, unconscious, psychic mechanisms, separation of the affect from its idea, etc.,—we might easily imagine ourselves to be in a circle of psycho-analysts, and yet it has never occurred to these investigators to ask themselves whether, after these experiences in the war neuroses, the psycho-analytical concepts cannot be made use of in the explanation of the usual neuroses and psychoses which were well known to us in peace times. The specificity of the war trauma is universally denied; in general, it is said, that the war neuroses contain nothing and have added nothing new to the already known symptomatology of the neuroses; even the Munich Congress of German Neurologists formally demanded the elimination of the word and concept, "war neurosis". If, however, the peace and war neuroses are identical in their nature, then neurologists will be obliged to make use of all these ideas of emotional shock, of the fixation of pathogenic memories, and of their continued activity in the unconscious, etc., also in the explanation of the usual hysterias, the obsessional neuroses and the psychoses. They will be astonished how easy it will be for them to traverse the path trodden by Freud, and will regret having shown such obstinate resistance to his hints.

To the question of the disposition to fall sick with a war neurosis the authors gave contradictory answers. Most of them follow the views of Gaupp, Laudenheimer and others, according to whom most of the war neurotics are *ab ovo* neuropaths or psychopaths, the shock merely playing the part of the releasing factor. Bonhoeffer says direct: "The possibility of a psychopathological condition being evoked by psychogenic factors is the criterion of a degenerative predisposition". Forster and Jendrassik say the same thing. Nonne, on the contrary, finds that the deciding factor in falling a victim to war neuroses lies less in the personal constitution than in the nature of the operating injury. Psycho-analysis takes a median position with regard to this question, which Freud has frequently and expressly stated. It speaks of an "aetiological succession" in the predisposition, the traumatic occasion figuring as reciprocal value with this. A trifling predisposition and severe shock can produce the same effects as an increased predisposition and a much lesser degree of shock. Psycho-analysis, however, is not content with the theoretical allusion to this condition, but it endeavours—with success—to separate the complex idea of the "disposition" into simpler elements and establish those constitutional factors that influence the choice of neurosis (the special tendency to fall sick with this or that neurosis). I shall return later to the question as to where psycho-analysis looks for the special disposition to falling sick with a traumatic neurosis.

The literature concerning the symptomatology of the neuroses of the war is simply immense. According to Gaupp, for example, the following hysterical symptoms are to be observed. "Attacks of a slight nature up to those of the severest kind, with an *arc de cercle* lasting for hours, sometimes with epileptic frequency, astasia-abasia, anomalies of the position and movement of the body even to going on all fours, all the varieties of tic and shaking tremors, paralyses and contractures in monoplegic, hemiplegic and paraplegic forms, deafness and deaf and dumbness, stuttering and stammering, aphonia and rhythmical screaming, blindness with or without blepharo-spasm, all kinds of disturbances of sensation, and most of all twilight states in quantities never before met with and in combination with phenomena of physical irritation and disorders". You see, it is like a museum of glaring hysterical symptoms, and whoever has once seen it will plainly have to decline Oppenheim's view, according to which purely neurotic symptoms are rarely seen in the traumatic neuroses of the war. Schuster draws attention to the frequent vasomotor and trophic phenomena; according to him, these are no longer psychogenic. Psycho-analysis, however, will agree with those who hold that these symptoms can originate to some extent from psychic causes, analogous to the physical alterations which can be produced under hypnosis. Finally, all the authors allude to the alterations in disposition, apathy and over-excitability, etc. after the trauma.

Out of this chaos of symptoms the "trembling" neurosis stands out through its frequency and conspicuousness. You all know those pathetic creatures who hobble along through the streets with shaking knees, uncertain gait and peculiar motor disturbances. They give the impression of being helpless and incurable invalids; and yet experience shows that also this traumatic form of illness is purely psychogenic. A single treatment with electricity and suggestion, a few hypnotic sittings are often sufficient in rendering these men capable of doing some work, if only temporarily and under certain conditions. Erben has made the most careful investigation into these disturbances of innervation; he found that these disturbances are only suspended or increased when the respective group of muscles carry out an action or intend to do so. His explanation for this is, that here the "volitional impulse makes a path for the spasm", which, however, is only the physiological paraphrase of the facts of the case. Psycho-analysis suspects here a psychical motivation: the activity of an unconscious contrary wish which puts itself in the way of the consciously wished act. This is indeed most striking in those patients of Erben who are prevented from going forward through the most violent attacks of shaking, but can carry out the much more difficult task of going backwards without trembling. Erben also here has a complicated physiological explanation ready, but forgets that the movement backwards, which removes the patient from the dangerous goal of the forward movement—and finally from the front line—does not need to be disturbed by any contrary wish. The remaining kinds of motor disturbances demand a similar interpretation, in particular the striking, uncontrollable running of many neurotics, so like the propulsion in paralysis agitans. These are the men who do not recover from the effect of the terror and are still always flying from dangers to which they were once exposed.

Many investigators, including non-psycho-analysts, came to the conclusion from these and similar observations, that these disturbances are not the direct effects of the trauma, but psychical reactions to it and act in the service of the instinct of self-preservation against the repetition of the unpleasant occurrence. We know that also the normal organism has at its disposal such protective measures. The symptoms of the terror, such as the immovable legs, the tremblings, the hesitating speech, seem to be useful automatisms; one is reminded by them of certain animals which simulate being dead when danger threatens. And if Bonhoeffer looks upon these traumatic disturbances as fixations of the means of expression of the terrible emotion which has been suffered, Nonne goes further and discovers that "the hysterical symptoms represent partly a reminiscence of inborn guard and defence mechanisms, the suppression of which in those individuals whom we call hysterical has not taken place in the normal degree or not at all". According to Hamburger the most frequently occurring type of disturbances of standing, walking and speech associated with shaking tremors represents a "complex of ideas of feebleness, weakness, refusal and exhaustion", and Gaupp sees in the same symptoms the lapse into infantile and puerile states of obvious helplessness. Some authors actually speak of the "fixation" in the traumatic posture of the body and innervation.

It cannot escape the notice of anyone with a knowledge of psycho-analysis how near these authors, without knowing it, are to psycho-analysis. The "expressions of fixations of movements" described by them are in reality only paraphrases of the Breuer-Freudian hysterical conversion, and the lapse into atavistic and infantile methods of reaction is nothing more nor less than what Freud called special attention to as the regressive character of the neurotic symptoms, all of which according to him only signify reversions into ontogenetic and phylogenetic stages of development already overcome. At any rate we have definite proof that neurologists have now decided to *interpret* certain nervous symptoms, that is to say, refer them to unconscious psychical contents, which would never have occurred to anyone to do before the introduction of psycho-analysis.

I will now speak of the few authors who occupy themselves with the war neuroses from the psycho-analytical points of view.

Stern has published a work on the psycho-analytical treatment of the war neuroses in war hospitals. I have not been able to see the work in the original, but I learn from the abstracts that the author proceeds from the point of view of repression and finds the situation of the serving soldier particularly suited to the production of neuroses in consequence of the suppression of affects which his service demands. Schuster admits that the investigations of Freud "however one may feel towards them" have thrown a ray of light on the psycho-genesis of the neuroses; they assist in revealing the hidden connection between symptom and psychical content which still exists though difficult to discover. Mohr treats the war neuroses by the cathartic method of Breuer and Freud, by getting the patients to live through the critical scenes again and brings about an abreaction of their affects by letting them re-experience the terrible emotion. Simmel is the only one up to the present who has occupied himself methodically with the psycho-catharsis of the war neuroses, and he will give his own report of his experiences to the Congress. Finally, I will mention my own investigations concerning the psychology of the war neuroses, in which I made the attempt to bring the traumatic forms of disorder into the category of psycho-analysis.

In this connection I will allude to a discussion which branches out in all directions on the question whether an affect can still act psycho-genetically when the person concerned immediately loses consciousness. Goldscheider and many others still maintain that a psychical effect is made impossible through swooning, and Aschaffenburg adheres to the view that loss of consciousness before falling ill guards against the neurosis. Nonne rightly opposes this view, and points out that unconscious mental streams could act psychically in spite of the loss of consciousness. L. Mann, relying on Breuer's hypnoidal theory, puts forward the view that the loss of consciousness before falling ill does not protect but disposes to the appearance of the neurosis, by preventing the discharge of the affects. Orlovsky expresses himself the most rationally on this vexed question; he points out the possibility that the swooning itself can be a psychogenic symptom, a flight into unconsciousness, which would spare the person concerned the conscious experiencing of the painful situation and sensations.

The possibility of the psychogenic formation of symptoms during a faint is quite comprehensible to those of us who are psycho-analysts. This problem could be started only by authors who take up a standpoint, obsolete to psycho-analysis, that equates mental with conscious.

I do not know, ladies and gentlemen, whether you also have obtained the impression from all these quotations and references (which are only taken at random from the literature) that an advance, even though one that is not admitted, has taken place in the attitude of leading neurologists towards the teachings of psycho-analysis. Moreover, candid recognition is not lacking; for example, the expression of Nonne, that Freud's experiences concerning the elaboration in the unconscious have received interesting illuminations and corroborations through the experiences of the war.

However, the same sentence of acknowledgement also contains a nihilistic opinion of Nonne concerning psycho-analysis; he states that Freud's idea of the almost exclusively sexual foundation of hysteria has been conclusively disproved during the war. We can no longer leave this unanswered, which after all is only a partial denial of psycho-analysis: also we can very easily give the answer. The war neuroses, according to psycho-analysis, belong to a group of neuroses in which not only is the genital sexuality affected, as in ordinary hysteria, but also its precursor, the so-called narcissism, self-love, just as in dementia praecox and paranoia. I grant that the sexual foundation of these so-called narcissistic neuroses is less easily apparent, particularly to those who equate sexuality and genitality and have neglected to use the word "sexual" in the sense of the old platonic Eros. Psycho-analysis, however, returns to this extremely ancient standpoint when it treats all tender and sensual relations of the man to his own or to the opposite sex, emotional feelings towards friends, relatives and fellow-creatures generally, even the affective behaviour towards one's own ego and body, partly under the rubric "erotism", otherwise "sexuality". It cannot be denied that those to whom this idea is strange cannot so easily be convinced of the correctness of Freud's postulation of the sexual theory in a narcissistic neurosis in particular, for example, in the traumatic neurosis. We should like to advise them to examine themselves into the usual (non-traumatic) hysteria and obsessional neuroses also, and to keep strictly to the methods of free association, dream and symptom interpretation proposed by Freud; then they will be much more easily convinced of the correctness of the sexual theories of the neuroses, and agreement about the sexual background of the war neuroses will follow. At any rate the triumph concerning the overthrow of the sexual theories is somewhat premature.

The observation that I have made as regards the participation of sexual factors in the formation of symptoms in the traumatic neuroses also shows that in traumatic neurotics the genital sexual hunger (libido) and potency is generally greatly injured; in many cases it can even be entirely suspended and that for long periods. This condition which is a positive one is alone sufficient to demonstrate the rashness of Nonne's conclusion[3].

Ladies and gentlemen: With what I have said I have discharged the chief task of my paper, which was the critical survey of the literature on the war neuroses from the standpoint of psycho-analysis. However, I will make use of this rare opportunity to tell you some of the observations I have made myself, and I will present points of view which may help to explain these conditions psycho-analytically.

In the psychical sphere of the traumatic neuroses there predominate such symptoms as hypochondriacal depression, terror, anxiousness, and a high degree of irritability with a tendency to outbursts of anger. Most of these symptoms can be traced back to *increased ego-sensitiveness* (in particular the hypochondria and the incapability of tolerating physical or mental discomfort). This over-sensitiveness arises from the fact that in consequence of the shock, which has been experienced once or repeatedly, the interest and sexual hunger (libido) of the patients is withdrawn from the object into the ego. There thus comes about a damming-up of the sexual hunger (libido) in the ego, which is expressed in those abnormal hypochondriacal organic sensations and over-sensitiveness. Frequently this heightened

---

[3] These facts have been confirmed in the course of the conference by all taking part in the discussions.

ego-love degenerates into a kind of infantile narcissism: the patients would like to be pampered, cared for, and pitied like children. One can therefore speak of a reversion into the childish stage of self-love. This heightening corresponds to the diminution of object-love, often also of genital potency. A man who is already predisposed to narcissism will of course sooner fall a victim to a traumatic neurosis; still no one is entirely immune from it, since the stage of narcissism forms a significant fixation point in the development of the sexual hunger (libido) of every human being. The combination with other narcissistic neuroses, especially paranoia and dementia, frequently occurs.

The symptom of anxiety is the sign of the shock to the self-confidence occasioned by the trauma. This is most strikingly expressed in men who, in consequence of an explosion, have been knocked down, hurled over or blown up and have thereby permanently lost their self-confidence. The characteristic disturbances of walking (astasia-abasia with trembling) are protective measures against the repetition of the anxiety, therefore phobias in Freud's sense. The cases in which these symptoms predominate are called anxiety-hysteria. Those symptoms, on the contrary, which simply express the situation at the moment of the explosion (innervation, position of the body) are conversion-hysterias in the psycho-analytical sense. Also in the anxiety there is naturally a constitutional predisposition; those persons more easily fall ill in this way who, in spite of real cowardice, are compelled from ambition to perform courageous deeds. The anxiety-hysterical disturbance in walking is at the same time a reversion to an infantile stage of not-being-able-to-walk or of learning-to-walk.

Also the tendency to outbursts of rage and anger is a highly primitive method of reaction to a superior force; it can increase up to epileptic attacks, and represents more or less incoordinate discharges of affect analogous to those observed in the period of suckling. A milder variety of this loss of restraint is the lack of adaptation to discipline, which is practically never missing in the traumatic neuroses. The excessive need for love and the narcissism also give rise to this increased irritability.

The entire personality of most of the victims of trauma corresponds therefore to the child who is fretting, whimpering, unrestrained and naughty in consequence of a fright. The excessive importance which almost all the persons suffering from trauma attach to good food fits in with this picture. The slightest neglect in this respect may produce in them the most violent outbreaks of affect and even induce fits. Most of them are unwilling to work, they wish to be supported and provided for like a child.

It is here, therefore, not only a question, as Strümpell considers, of the production of illnesses on account of an actual gain (pension, compensation for injury, flight from the front) which are only secondary illness gains; the primary motive for the illness is the pleasure itself of remaining in the secure retreat of the childish situation once so unwillingly left behind. Both these narcissistic and apprehensive manifestations of illness have their atavistic prototype; it is even possible that the neurosis often reverts to methods of reaction which play no part at all in the individual development (feigning of death by animals, methods of progress and protection of the young of animals in the ancestral series). It is as though an over-strong affect could no longer be compensated along normal paths, but had to regress to previously abandoned but virtually existent mechanisms of reaction. I do not doubt that many other pathological reactions will yet be revealed as recapitulations of overcome methods of adaptation.

As symptoms of the traumatic neuroses which are less appreciated, I might mention the over-sensitiveness of all the senses (shunning of light, hyperacusis, extreme ticklishness) and the anxiety dreams. The real terrors that have been experienced, or things similar to them, are lived through again and again in these dreams. I am following a hint of Freud's when I look upon these terrors and anxiety dreams, as well as the state of terror by day, as spontaneous attempts of cure on the part of the patient. They serve to bring piecemeal to conscious abreaction the shock, which in its totality was intolerable and unintelligible and was therefore converted into symptoms, and to contribute to the adjustment of the disturbed equilibrium in the psychical economy.

Ladies and gentlemen, I hope these few remarks of mine may serve as proof that the psycho-analytical conception discloses points of view where the rest of neurology leaves us in the lurch.

From the methodical psycho-analysis of many cases we ought to expect the full explanation of these morbid conditions and perhaps also their radical cure.

While this article was in the press, I read the interesting work of Prof. E. Moro, the childrens' specialist of Heidelberg, on "the first Trimenon", *i. e.* the peculiarities of the first three months of the infant's life. He says: "If one lays a young infant on a pillow on a table and strikes the pillow on either side with the hands, then there results a peculiar reflex action. Both arms are thrown up symmetrically apart and then come together again in a curve with easy tonic movements. A similar movement is carried out simultaneously by the legs". We would say: Moro has here artificially produced a little shock (or traumatic) neurosis. The remarkable thing in this action is that this reflex to the shock in the young infant of less than three months old shows signs of the natural reflexes of clasping, which characterise the "carried offspring", *i. e.* the young of animals (monkeys) which are compelled with the help of a pronounced clasping reflex to hold fast with the fingers to the mother's fur while she climbs about the trees. We would say: Atavistic reversion of the method of reaction in sudden terror[4].

2. Dr. Karl Abraham, Berlin.

During the war academic neurologists have come round more and more to regard the aetiology of the traumatic neuroses from psychological points of view. However, in spite of the approach towards our views, mentioned by Ferenczi, their ideas differ from ours in two respects, namely, they for the most part only take into consideration the reactions of the ego impulses to the trauma, and they keep entirely to the manifest expressions of the neurosis. In the following remarks, besides those factors which we do not dispute, I intend to deal with the unconscious and sexual ones.

When in peace times psycho-analysis upheld the sexual aetiology of the neuroses it was often pointed out as a contrary argument that this could not hold good for the traumatic neuroses. Similarly now the opinion is expressed that the genesis of the war neuroses contravenes our ideas. Terror, anxiety lest the dangerous situation be repeated, seeking for a pension, and some vague idea of disposition are supposed to be adequate explanations of the illness; in the mass of the neuroses which have broken out during the war the unimportance of the sexual aetiology is thought to be clearly shown.

My investigations of the traumatic neuroses in peace time had for a long time led me to conclude the importance of sexuality in them similar to that in the other neuroses, but they have not yet been sufficiently numerous and conclusive enough for publication. I might mention the case of a young girl who met with a slight tram accident when she was in the throes of a serious erotic conflict. The analysis showed that the accident in a certain measure gave a pretext for the outbreak of the neurosis. The symptoms were in connection with the conflict in question; the importance of the trauma receded quite into the background. I might also add that some litigious cases of traumatic neurosis which I observed in greater detail all suffered from impotence; this disturbance was produced by the accident, but seemed to have its real basis in old and unconscious sexual resistances.

The investigation of war neurotics has fully confirmed my surmises connected with such observations. Moreover, the recurrence of certain definite symptoms in war neurotics, which were familiar to me not only in the traumatic neuroses of peace time, but also in the non-traumatic cases, seems to me worth noting. I refer particularly to the complex of symptoms which we could so often observe during the war in the anxiety cases with trembling, such as trembling, agitation, irritability, sensitiveness, sleeplessness, headaches, anxiety, depression of spirits and feelings of incompetency. Two neurotic types with the same symptoms—although these do not appear so prominently as in the war—would be the impotent man and the frigid woman. A similarity which is so marked in external phenomena leads one to expect a similarity also in internal processes.

[4] (*"Münchner Mediz. Wochenschrift"* No. 42, P. 1150.)

All my experience fully coincides with that which Ferenczi has just communicated. The trauma acts on the sexuality of many persons in the sense that it gives the impulse to a regressive alteration which endeavours to reach narcissism. I might add that we both arrived at this idea without having previously even mentioned it to one another. The trauma, however, has this effect only in a portion of those participating in the war, hence we are unable to dispense with the assumption of an individual disposition, but we are in the position to define it far more accurately than the prevailing school of neurology. A couple of examples will make the problem before us clearer.

At the beginning of the war a soldier at the front was wounded on August, 12th, 1914. Before his wound was completely healed he secretly left the hospital and went again to the front, soon getting a second and after a few months a third wound. After repeated returns to the front he was one day blown up by a shell explosion and was unconscious for two days. After these four traumata he certainly presented the phenomena following upon shock, but no neurotic picture, being neither particularly anxious, depressed nor excited. Another man at the front during a night attack fell into a hole without injuring himself, but immediately developed neurotic trembling of a most severe kind, and presented the picture of a mental breakdown. How are such differences to be explained?

The previous history of such people, and naturally, still more, a penetrating analysis, teaches us why the one in spite of the severest physical and mental influences of the war remains to all intents and purposes healthy, and why the other reacts to relatively trifling stimuli with a severe neurosis. It transpires with great regularity that the war neurotics already before the trauma were labile people—to designate it, to begin with, by a general expression—and especially so as regards their sexuality. Many of these men were unable to carry out their tasks in practical life, others that were capable of doing this, however, showed little initiative and manifested little impelling energy. In all of them sexual activity was diminished, their sexual hunger (libido) being checked through fixations; in many of them already before the campaign potency was weak or they were only potent under certain conditions. Their attitude towards the female sex was more or less disturbed through partial fixation of the sexual hunger (libido) in the developmental stage of narcissism. Their sexual and social capacity of functioning was dependent on their making certain concessions to their narcissism.

In the war these men were placed under completely changed conditions and in the face of extraordinary demands. They had always to be prepared for unconditional self-sacrifice in favour of the mass. This signifies the renunciation of all narcissistic privileges. The healthy person is able to accomplish such a complete suppression of his narcissism: he loves according to the transference type, and so is capable of sacrificing his ego for the whole. In this respect those disposed to neuroses are inferior to healthy persons.

It is not only demanded of these men in the field that they must tolerate dangerous situations—a purely passive performance—but there is a second demand which has been much too little considered, I allude to the aggressive acts for which the soldier must be hourly prepared, for besides the readiness to die, the readiness to kill is demanded of him.

A further factor which operates on the labile sexuality of those disposed to neuroses is the almost exclusive association with men. The sexuality of the normal person takes no harm from this, but it is otherwise in men with strong narcissistic traits. The knowledge of the connection between homosexuality and narcissism enables us to understand this.

The previously unstable attitude towards women begins to waver under such conditions. If the lability of the attitude towards the other sex is very great then it does not need even a war trauma to cause a neurosis to break out in such men. For instance, I observed a man who on return from furlough at home had a convulsive attack and was brought into the hospital showing signs of anxiety and depression. The man had always been noted for his effeminate disposition, and in his married life was weakly potent and always inclined to jealousy. When he was home on leave he failed absolutely in the attempt to have sexual relations with his wife. His fears that his wife would be unfaithful to him reached a crisis, and soon after his departure from home he had his convulsive attack.

Such men with labile heterosexual impulses need a support for their sexuality. They frequently find this in their wife on whom their sexual hunger (libido) is completely dependent, or they have to defend themselves from their feelings of insecurity sexually by having constantly to convince themselves that they are potent by going with prostitutes. And so in war they constantly need a support for their wavering activity. Their military usefulness also is dependent upon conditions. They are frequently useful in rank and file, supporting their activity upon that of their comrades. A changed situation, and occurrence, which with a marked disposition needs only to be very trifling, upsets the balance, making the previously weakly-active man wholly passive. The passivity is expressed then not only in the sphere of the ego impulses, but likewise in that of the sexual impulses. The narcissism breaks out. The capability of the transference of the sexual hunger (libido) dies away as well as the capacity of self-sacrifice in favour of the community. On the contrary, we now have a patient before us who himself needs care and consideration on the part of others, who in a typically narcissistic manner is in constant anxiety about his life and health. The obtrusiveness of the symptoms (tremors, attacks, etc.) is also narcissistic. Many of the patients show themselves completely female-passive in the surrender to their suffering. In their symptoms they are experiencing anew the situation which had caused the neurosis to break out, and soliciting the sympathy of other people.

At this juncture we must again refer to the previously mentioned circumstance that in our patients the anxiety as regards killing is of a similar significance to that of dying. The symptoms in part are only comprehensible in this sense. The case of a man who in the field suffered from a relapse of a neurosis which he had had six years previously is especially instructive. At that time he was taken with a tremor of his arm which arose in connection with a dream in which he murdered someone; a hand-to-hand fight in the field caused the old symptom to reappear. Hysterical convulsive attacks are not only produced through dangerous situations, terror, etc., but not infrequently an act of aggression which he has failed to carry out is expressed in them. Such an attack is especially often associated with an exchange of words with his superiors; the suppressed impulse to forcible activity finds in the expression its motor discharge.

The complete instability of many war neurotics, their disconcerting depression, their propensity to thoughts of death, find a further explanation in a particular effect of the trauma. Many of the neurotically disposed persons, up to the moment when the trauma upsets them, have supported themselves only through an illusion connected with their narcissism, namely, through the belief in their immortality and invulnerability. The effect of an explosion, a wound, or things of a like nature suddenly destroys this belief. The narcissistic security gives way to a feeling of powerlessness and the neurosis sets in.

To what an extent the regression can go is shown in those cases, described also in the literature, in which the patients display the conduct of little children. One of my patients who was previously neurotic was thrown into this kind of condition through the terrifying effect of a mine explosion. For a long time he behaved like a terrified little child. For many weeks he could only reply to all questions about his trouble with the two words, "Mine bombs". He had therefore gone back to the mode of expression of a child hardly two years old.

What apparently is an exception to the statement made at the commencement is the following noteworthy case in which a previously healthy, proficient and sexually completely potent young man was taken in the field with a severe astasia-abasia coupled with a very great over-excitability of affect. An explosion had hurled the lower part of his back against the side of the trench; he had therefore suffered a trauma, and had been already treated by various neurologists for "traumatic hysteria". A careful physical examination showed me undoubted signs of an affection of the Conus Medullaris, manifestly a haematomyelia. The patient remembered that after the trauma he could not retain his urine and faeces, still he continued at his post because he looked upon this condition as the result of terror. These symptoms improved in the following weeks. However, during the same period he noticed the disappearance of all sexual feelings. At first he was not inclined to look upon this condition, which was disquietening to him, at all seriously, having no idea that he had an organic impotence. During leave at home he had to come to the conclusion that the sexual insensitiveness was in no way to be overcome. Now the neurosis appeared, not as the result of the psychic impression of the explosion, but as a reaction to the organic impotence of traumatic origin. This neurosis differed, by the way, from the usual traumatic neuroses through the euphoristic, at times even manic state of mind.

This difference needs special appreciation and explanation. Also other men who have received severe organic injuries show such mental attitudes which must surprise us. For example, I have always found that in the amputation hospitals a strikingly cheerful mood prevails. At the beginning of the war I had my attention drawn to the euphoria of the severely wounded men by a particular occurrence. I had to treat four soldiers in a general hospital, who through the splintering of the same shell had had their eyes severely injured. All four had already had enucleation performed in another hospital. They were in no way depressed but gave themselves up to a careless, serene frame of mind. When they—all at the same time—received their artificial eyes a remarkable scene took place. They jumped, danced, and laughed in boisterous spirits, just like children who work themselves up into a frenzy of joy. Also here there is without doubt a regression to narcissism, it is however of a more partial nature. These patients repress the knowledge that through the mutilation they have experienced a depreciation in a more or less high degree, especially in the eyes of the female sex. What they lose in love from outside they seek to compensate by means of self-love. The damaged part of the body receives for them a significance as an erotogenic zone which did not previously belong to it[5].

All the experiences here communicated speak unanimously in the sense that the war neuroses are not to be understood without taking the sexuality into consideration. This view receives a valuable confirmation by means of the mental disturbances observed in the war, which—like mental troubles in general—very often more easily manifest the latent content of their ideas than the neuroses. The mental disturbances which have broken out in the field, as other observers have confirmed, are associated only in a trifling part with the formation of delusions. However, if there is a delusion then it has even a manifest sexual content. In the cases I have seen the delusions are partly of jealousy, partly of homosexual persecution by comrades. I might mention the paranoid illness of a soldier which broke out when he, after long service in the field, went home on furlough and turned out to be impotent with his wife. A very transparent symbolism and other signs pointed with certainty to the significance of homosexual components as the fundamental cause of the delusion. Another man had the delusion of being, during sleep, infected with syphilis in the hospital by his comrades, the origin of the delusion was here also the result of imperfectly repressed homosexuality.

In this connection I should like to mention another remarkable case. In 1915 when I was acting at a surgical station a man was treated there for a gunshot wound of the penis. The operation, which was carried out by a well known surgeon, was quite successful. Two years later the same patient came to my psychiatric station. The man who was previously unaffected psychically now showed a paranoid mental disturbance. On questioning him it appeared that in consequence of the wound there existed entire genital anaesthesia. Also here the psychosis appeared to stand in close connection with the cessation of genital manliness.

The so-called "seeking for pension" of many men injured in the war is as little explained by means of the current ideas on the matter as the symptoms of the neurosis. This also stands in connection with the alterations of the sexual hunger (libido), just as do the neurotic symptoms. The patient only apparently fights for compensation for the stiffened wrist, for the shot-off finger, for his neurotic trouble. It is quite overlooked as a rule that the neurotic inwardly perceives the alteration which has taken place as regards his sexual hunger (libido). He is filled with the feeling of an enormous injury. And he is so far right when he actually has

---

[5] The hallucinations, which those persons who having had an amputation experience, that that part of the body which has been taken away is still there, might find an explanation from this source.

suffered loss from his capability for transference of his sexual hunger (libido) and therewith an important basis of the belief in himself. A man injured by an accident before the war once told me that he had come to an agreement with his insurance company for a definite compensation. Hardly had this occurred when the thought came to him that this sum did not even remotely cover his actual injury. Henceforth the sum which according to his idea he ought to have claimed rapidly rose to an enormous amount. The pension compensates only for the diminution of the capacity for earning a livelihood, so far as this is objectively demonstrable, not for that which the patient subjectively feels; he cannot be compensated for his reduced capacity for object-love. Narcissism also explains here the conduct of the patients. Where previously the capability of surrender (in every sense of the word) existed, now the narcissistic avarice dominates. The genital zone has lost its predominance; anal erotism is strengthened. It is clear that the state pension favours the development of the character traits described; this only takes place, however, when the tendency already exists in the injured person to react narcissistically to an external injury to his integrity.

Now as regards the question of the therapy and particularly that of the psycho-analytic.

At the commencement of the war one took little notice of the neurotics, they were placed perchance in a convalescent home but practically without treatment. The increasing number of neurotic cases necessitated other measures. The old method of "surprisal" was again dug up. Then came the period of "active" curative procedures, the best known of which is Kaufmann's. These methods were at first deceptive from the fact that they led to the rapid improvement of a great number of patients. As regards, however, the duration of the cure, they have not yielded what was hoped of them, and, in addition, they produced certain unwished-for phenomena. The military medical authorities therefore display a lively interest in putting on one side the too "active" methods in favour of other effective but less severe ones.

Is psycho-analysis able to step into the breach? Theoretically we are justified in assuming that it is, because psycho-analysis alone of all methods of treatment is a causal one. We also have already practical experience to go upon; I refer to the publications of Simmel. I will now briefly speak of my own therapeutic experiences. We psycho-analysts had to be extremely cautious in our treatment of war neuroses, for the addresses at medical congresses and the literature before the war had demonstrated very clearly the refusal of the medical profession to accept the conclusions of our ideas and efforts. When in 1916 I founded a station for neuroses and mental diseases I abstained entirely from all forcible therapy, likewise from hypnosis and other suggestive means, but allowed the patients to abreact in the waking state and sought to make intelligible to them by a kind of simplified psycho-analysis the origin and nature of their suffering. I aimed at arousing in the patients the feeling of being understood, complete relaxation, and improvement. Later the station became that of a pure observation station, chiefly for mental diseases; hence I could only collect isolated therapeutic experiences.

The objection that psycho-analysis works too slowly does not hold good as far as our experience goes up to the present.

Latterly it has appeared that the patients treated accordingly by the Kaufmann method frequently relapsed when they were withdrawn from the influence of the doctor, or were again exposed to the dangers of the front. Time will show whether the psycho-analytic methods will procure more lasting cures. I will communicate in conclusion the result, instructive in this connection, of the recent treatment of a neurosis carried out in my private practice. I was able in a few weeks to remove a severe phobia in a boy twelve years old, which referred to air raids. The cure persisted when the boy returned home; he was there again daily exposed to the risk of air raids and put up with this situation just like a healthy person. Perhaps this result justifies the expectation that psycho-analysis will in fact in the permanence of its cures fill up the gaps that exist at present. Psycho-analysis, which enables us to penetrate deeper than any other method into the structure of the war neuroses, will perhaps take therapeutic precedence also in the sphere of the war neuroses[6].

3. DR. ERNST SIMMEL, BERLIN.

FOR the past eighteen months I have been in charge of a special hospital for war neuroses, and the mass treatment necessary in such an institution has enabled me to make a comparative study of the different so-called psycho-therapeutic methods. Apart from the serious objections that can be raised with regard to all forcible and restrictive methods, which for the most part produce new psychic injuries, there are serious doubts as to the use of pure suggestion in the form of hypnosis when carried out indiscriminately as a blind technique for war neurotics. The removal of the symptom, which is done regardless of the remaining psychic constellations of the patient, generally produces at the same time a considerable general disturbance with marked subjective symptoms, such as headache, feelings of pressure on the head, insomnia, diminution of intellectual capacity, sexual impotence, etc.

On the other hand, the frequently observed fact that with the disappearance of the manifest symptom the neurosis appears in another form, has proved that with all these kinds of palliative measures the root cause of the suffering has not been touched.

A medical treatment that is to be effective can only be built up on the pathogenesis of a disease. The psycho-pathogenesis of the war neurosis, (and no intelligent man any longer doubts its psychic origin), obviously can be elucidated only by means of psycho-analysis. It is intelligible that a hospital regime necessitating the simultaneous treatment of a large number of cases and calling for rapid curative results, would allow a more extensive individual analysis only in a few cases. On account of this I had from the beginning to cut down the length of the treatment. A combination of analytical-cathartic hypnosis with analytical conversations during the waking state, and dream interpretation carried out both in the waking state and in deep hypnosis, has given me a method which on an average of two or three

[6] The intention of the medical department of the Prussian War Ministry in regard to the organisation of psycho-analytical treatment stations was not carried out in consequence of the altered political situation, which took place soon after the Congress.

sittings brought about relief of the symptoms. This mode of treatment implies a systematic investigation of the symptoms that have appeared in consequence of the incongruity of the war experience and the psychic preparedness of the patient; such investigation being both aetiologically conditioned as to its nature and automatically effective as to its working. With the disappearance of the symptoms the essential treatment of the war neurotics, according to modern hospital methods, was looked upon as being at an end. An analytical cure of the entire personality by a shortened and combined method will have to be reserved for the psychological clinic of the future.

The psycho-analytical explanation of the war neuroses has proved with wonderful clearness the correctness of the Freudian views on hysteria, according to which all physical symptoms represent conversions of something psychical. The body is the instrument of the mind upon which it (the mind) allows its unconscious to manifest itself in plastic and mimic expression. The functions of the unconscious are the deciding factor in the formation and building up of the war neuroses, also the frequently observed instances of the forgetting of events accompanied by feelings hostile to the ego, even when these events are very recent, permits us to recognise from the outside alone the submergence and repression of ideas and affects of a painful nature. It is comprehensible that under the pressure of years of discipline, which limits the personality and thereby prevents every individual reaction to events, the disposition to repression is extraordinarily favoured. To what degree an enforced sexual abstinence further increases this could not be tested.

The unconscious meaning of the *symptoms* of the war neurotics, as we may state by anticipation, is for the most part of a non-sexual nature, there being exhibited in them all those war-produced affects of terror, anxiety, rage, etc. associated with ideas corresponding with the actual occurrences of the war. Stekel is quite wrong in concluding from my statements that I categorically deny a sexual basis for neuroses in general, since at present only the *symptomatology* of the war neuroses is explained on the basis of these analytical investigations. The fact of the predisposition to neuroses is still a long way from being exhausted. The fact that in the midst of the self-same experiences one soldier remains well while another becomes a neurotic may, so far as my experience goes, be very well connected with the psycho-sexual constellation of the particular person. The systematic investigation of the dream-life of the soldier, even after the removal of the war neurotic symptoms, has indeed made it possible to recognise quite frequently threads that lead down to the primordial network of infantile sexuality. Also many soldiers who have broken down solely under the pressure of discipline show even in this abortive form of analysis an attitude of father defiance in consequence of an infantile mother fixation as the subconscious condition of their need for opposition. In some cases even the sexual trauma of childhood becomes evident as the latent basis of the war neurosis just in the quick and deep view which is gained by hypnosis in the combined form of treatment. The war affects and ideas which form the symptoms have, on the other hand, a certain intrinsic relation to sexuality inasmuch as they are closely bound with the most primitive instincts in man,—those connected with the self-preservation instinct. If the sexual affect in the last resort originates in the instinct which is directed towards the preservation of the species, the affects of anxiety, horror, rage, etc. produced by the war are connected with the elementary urging of the preservation of the individual, and not, as superficial observers imagine, solely for the purpose of preserving the physical existence, but above all that of the psychic existence.

The war neuroses are essentially interposed guarantees, the object of which is to protect the soldier against a psychosis. Anyone who has examined a great number of patients for eighteen months with perception that has been analytically sharpened, must recognise that the proportionately small number of war psychoses is only to be explained by the proportionately large number of war neuroses.

One must have experienced the war occurrences themselves or their recapitulation under analytical-cathartic hypnosis in order to understand to what attacks the mental life of a man is exposed in time of war. For instance, a man after being wounded several times has to return to the front, or is separated from important events in his family for an indefinite time, or finds himself exposed irretrievably to that murderous monster, the tank, or to an enemy gas attack which is rolling towards him; again, shot and wounded by shrapnel he has often to lie for hours or days among the gory and mutilated bodies of his comrades, and, not least of all, his self-respect is sorely tried by unjust and cruel superiors who are themselves dominated by complexes, yet he has to remain calm and mutely allow himself to be overwhelmed by the fact that he has no individual value, but is merely one unimportant unit of the whole.

It is now explicable why the war neurosis of the officer does not generally exhibit such gross symptoms as that of the ordinary soldier. The officer has raised himself above the crowd, and, with a higher mental development, has more possibilities of individually sublimating his own particular injuries. Nevertheless, the neuroses in officers will claim our psycho-therapeutic treatment in a far higher degree as soon as our colleagues agree not to look upon them from moral standpoints and to consider their comrades of the officer class under the courtesy diagnoses of Neurasthenia, Ischia, Neuralgia, etc.

The war neurosis, like the peace neurosis, is the expression of a splitting of the personality. The conditions for such a splitting are brought about by the consistent narrowing of the personality complex as a result of the compulsory discipline and above all by the psychic and physical exhaustion of one or more years of war. The soldier severely burdened with undischarged mental material is compelled to meet abnormally heavy demands. An accident or a disastrous event then causes the obstructed personality to break down. Complexes with accentuated feelings held down in the unconscious become unduly powerful, and the neurosis becomes manifest. The passage from the psychical to the physical, however, signifies here more than a self-preserving process of the psyche. The act of falling ill is, in my opinion, at the same time the commencement of the healing process. The consistent use of analytic hypnosis has repeatedly shown that the physical symptoms in their mute expression strive to bring to the notice of the man the elements that are disturbing his personality and which are imprisoned and obstructed in his unconscious. Since the union between conscious and unconscious is interrupted within by the strong barrier of the resistance, a detour by way of external physical paths is necessary in order to re-establish the harmonious fitting together of the personality.

If the predominant physical symptoms of the war neuroses are modes of expression of unconsciously determined ideas, the more psychic forms of these neuroses, the states of inhibition or excitement, are due to an effort on the part of the repressed affects to re-establish the disturbed psychic balance. A strict demarcation between aetiologically effective ideas and sensations is naturally not conceivable. The relationship can only be a quantitative one. All ideas obviously stand in a quite special relationship to the ego of the patient through their accentuation of feelings; on the other hand, the affects are bound to their causative ideas.

The first part of our mental analytic therapy is to recognise the meaning of the neurotic healing tendency, the second, to convey our knowledge to the patient. The crowning point of our treatment consists in securing the spontaneous cooperation of the neurotic who, freed of his emotional inhibition, and now in harmony with himself, has, through his wider mental field of vision, a greater scope for the activity of his will power. Man can only desire what he knows. By reason of this the analyst comes to realise that the diagnosis, "mala voluntas", which so often brings the doctor who is untrained in analysis into conflict with his patient, mostly betokens a "mala potentia" of the doctor who knows nothing about the functions of the unconscious.

The weakening of the personality complexes of the soldier, as just described, his subjection to other ideas with accentuated feelings which are held down in the subconscious and thus connected with the constant readiness to subordination under the strivings of ego-hostile feelings, represents the so-called morbid suggestibility. To make use of this suggestibility for curative purposes without exposing its foundations is to increase the illness instead of bringing about a cure.

The neurotic, in my opinion, succumbs in the first instance to auto-suggestion, that is to say, to over-strong emotionally toned ideas which have arisen in him at a time when the ego-complex is weakened in power or completely suspended.

According to my observations, narrowings and suppressions of consciousness represent the initial stages of the war neuroses. In the smallest loss of consciousness, the shock effects of terror, up to the severe fainting attacks and the long continued loss of consciousness after being buried, we see the self-conscious of the personality more or less obliterated and the way opened to the unconscious. Here undoubtedly at the commencement are operating those teleological mechanisms which constitute the foundation of the neuroses and their formation of symptoms. Consciousness refuses to take up ideas or to assimilate at the moment those things which are too horrible in their reality to be consciously tolerated. Therefore those psychic shocks, those fainting attacks and profound loss of consciousness denote, provided there is no injury *in cerebro*, a power of the unconscious that attracts to itself the entire psychosis in a salutary manner.

Hypnosis gives us a clear picture of these processes. It shows us the patient in the same state of consciousness as that in which during the war he had acquired the origin of the illness. During hypnosis the soldier relates, or once again lives through, all the things that he had experienced in former circumstances only unconsciously. We learn of distressing pains of which, when he was buried, he never became conscious. In such a hypnosis we see his anxiety displayed, his anger arise, feelings which at the moment of the excitation were benumbed and like lightning were dragged violently into the unconscious.

I can best illustrate what I have said by a few examples. For instance, the simplest cases, which occurred so often, of a flaccid paralysis of the arm after a slight gunshot wound that had been well healed for a long time and which seemed to be of a purely physical nature, showed its unconscious connections very quickly in one sitting. Consciousness only knows, "I cannot move my arm", and no amount of reasoning was of any avail. However, the unconscious spoke during hypnosis: "In the excitement of the attack my mind became a blank. When I was hit the impact of the shrapnel was so great that my arm felt as though it was pulled violently backwards, and I immediately thought it was torn off". The correction of the unconscious idea in hypnosis which again united the idea of the torn off arm with consciousness here quickly settled the question of an organic basis of the symptom, It can be easily understood that an arm which is no longer recognised as existing is also completely analgesic.

The neurotic symptoms which owe their origin to such suddenly occurring events we can consequently regard in their effects as realised post-hypnotic auto-suggestions. I have confirmed this view by numerous examples, I might mention the case of a soldier who suffered from a severe facial tic by which he was constantly making a grimace, and who at the same time had a contracture of the right knee joint, both of which symptoms had proved quite refractory to the usual treatment by suggestion. Hypnosis, which restored the conscious situation of the initial blowing up, very soon yielded the following information. While the patient lay unconscious under a wreckage of stones and while scenes of his native place appeared to him as in a dream, he was constantly compelled to make grimaces in order to remove the mass of sand which lay on his face and also for the purpose of breathing freely. At the same time a sharp stone was pressing on his right heel which compelled him to keep his leg bent. This compulsion which was united with unconscious ideas acted therefore as a post-hypnotic suggestion for more than a year afterwards, until at last the command which the unconscious had imposed on the patient could be annulled during hypnosis by means of my correction. In this way was the removal of these symptoms brought about. I could quote further similar examples in which these kinds of contractures represent a compulsory holding of a part in a position of ease which is based on unconscious sensations of pain.

Apart from repressed physical sensations of pain the affects themselves also naturally play an important part in the neurotic compulsion to maintain a particular position, I remember a soldier who for several months had a compulsion to keep both eyes fixed and turned upwards and to the left. This symptom failed to react to methods of suggestion. Analysis under hypnosis within a few minutes gave the explanation and at the same time the removal of the symptom. The patient had anxiously expected the falling down of trunks of trees from above and to the left through the bursting of shells during a drum fire. His eyes became fixed in dread before the fate threatening him. The original situation had in the meantime become unreal, nevertheless the anxiety in itself was valid. The patient was still a soldier and retained in his neurosis the anxiety—an anxiety of similar situations. The neurosis of another soldier, which for a long time had been considered of an organic nature, a bulbar paralysis being suspected, was very instructive and the success of the treatment most gratifying. This man in addition to an apparently harmless superficial gunshot wound of the back suffered from a spasm of the muscles of the throat, a dysphagia, that made it impossible for him to take solid food, while liquid food was only possible in small quantities. The spasm of the throat and muscles of mastication turned out to be "suppressed rage". This soldier who was cut off when on patrol was stealing alone through a wood when he saw a comrade being ill-treated by Frenchmen on the main road. This scene he reproduced fully and dramatically under hypnosis in which he stealthily crawled about, ground his teeth together and gnashed them in impotent rage over the scene which he had witnessed. At that time he was struck in the back by a chance shot which caused him to faint for a short time. He then succeeded in getting back to his company and was sent into hospital on account of his superficial wound. The living through this scene again with its accompanying emotions completely freed him from his dysphagia. This example also shows how repressed rage manifests itself as a more positive feeling tone through physical increase of tonus in contrast to the previously described cases with negative and depressed accentuation of feelings which are physically represented by a lowering of tone and in flaccid paralyses. Here an opportunity may be taken of alluding to the fact that one can demonstrate without difficulty during hypnosis the displacement from the psychical into the physical. If we interrupt the patient in the abreaction of his rage during hypnosis then he reacts with a general tremor or the tremor of an extremity which is already in some way psychically affected.

Further I might mention the case of a neurotic who suffered from a shaking tremor of the right arm with peculiar circular movements of the thumb and fore-finger. This tremor had been removed by pure suggestive methods, but one morning it returned, as the patient expressed it "by itself". On closer questioning he remembered that the shaking had re-appeared in conjunction with a terrifying dream during the previous night; the actual content of the dream he had forgotten. During hypnosis the patient immediately became conscious again of the dream, and by means of it of those events which still compelled him to shake his arm. During the night he had dreamed of a Russian with a black beard who sprang on to his bed in order to strangle him. He awoke in anxiety and terror with his arm shaking. The patient had seen the face of this Russian appear over the parapet during a furious hand grenade fight just when he was on the point of fixing a grenade fuse and was suddenly blown over. He lost consciousness with his rage undischarged and an incipient movement which served as a mimic abreaction of this anger.

From this example, to which I could add many more, it becomes evident that dream material directly forces itself on the attention of the intelligent psycho-therapeutists as of great assistance in the treatment of war neuroses.

I do not treat any patients whose dreams I do not know. I have learnt for a long time now to estimate the dreams of my war neurotic patients as an attempt at self-healing, especially in the psycho-cathartic sense. I never give drugs for the dreams of anxiety, terror and rage. I am glad of the cooperation of the patient, I learn by listening to his dreams his own tendency to cure, then I get him to continue the dream under hypnosis where it has stopped the previous night, or, this I have several times found successful, I cause the patient to continue in his dreams at night from where the hypnosis has left off. Incidentally it may be remarked that after all these experiences I look upon hypnosis not as an artificial sleep but as a definite stage of natural sleep, which by virtue of its artificial induction enables one to maintain a direct rapport with the sleeper.

The initial stage of auto-hypnosis, hypnosis, and dreams represents the same *niveau* as that in which the germs of the illness lie embedded and can be removed.

In corroboration of this view I might mention a patient who was in a stuporose condition, with paralysis of all the limbs, and who was also almost deaf and dumb. By means of suggestion *en masse, i.e.* when lying down among other patients who were being hypnotised, it at length became possible to hypnotise him. Even then the patient remained completely stuporose. Only when his sister succeeded in getting from him a few words concerning an anxiety dream, and after I had repeated these words to him during hypnosis did marked excitation take place in the stuporose man. The unconscious became sensitised and with effective discharge came the recapitulation of the causative occurrence. The patient having been forced by some jealous and stronger companions to drag along some branches of trees was overturned into a mass of mud in which he threatened to suffocate. The subconscious idea was that his mouth and ears were filled with mud and his limbs pressed into it. During hypnosis he cleared away this imaginary mud with all his might.

There are, on the other hand, patients who inversely take over the impulse for curative discharge from the hypnosis into the dream. A young lieutenant assisted thus very practically in the reduction of his pent-up affects. For weeks after being blown up he was mentally deranged and delirious, and still suffered from states of excitement being unable to carry out the simplest intellectual processes, such as counting, reading, etc. After the first hypnosis which brought about a recapitulation of the most recent occurrences with a corresponding discharge of affect, there followed an intense fury dream. The patient wrenched out several iron bars from his bed and battered the wall with them. In the dream he was striking a canal worker with them whom he had seen daily from the window of the hospital. The conversation next morning showed that the canal worker had the features of an orderly who had wanted to detain him in the field hospital and thus prevent him going back to the front to avenge his brother. The patient's brother had recently been killed whilst serving in the same regiment, and the lieutenant had been fighting with fury and grief in order to avenge him when he was blown up. His first delirious attack had been directed against this particular orderly.

Sometimes one succeeded in directly stimulating the self-treatment of the patient in the dream. I recollect a neurotic who suffered from a severe disturbance of speech and also of walking, the result of a spastic paralysis of the legs and muscles of the mouth in consequence of a strong repression of rage. The discharge which took place under hypnosis was so dangerous to those in the vicinity that I had prematurely to break off the treatment. However, before waking the patient I told him to discharge the unreleased part in his dream. I let him sleep alone with an orderly. In the middle of the night he sprang up and again lived through an experience of anxiety and rage accompanied with shouting and raving, and although previously paralysed he ran down the whole length of the staircase of the hospital.

An especially frequent symptom in the war neuroses—the convulsive attacks—directly represents, in my opinion, an auto-hypnotic state appearing in the form of an attack.

Being buried (as the result of an explosion) with its total obliteration of the conscious ego, naturally the most frequent originator of the war neuroses, acts most often as the first cause. The loss of consciousness during the convulsive attack and the subsequent amnesia is that beneficent not-knowing into which the neurotic person flies before the memory of that all too horrible situation, or before the knowledge of some act of his own which he may have to perform as a result of his affective damming-up, but which nevertheless brings him into grave danger. I have already in my earlier work alluded to the fact that the physical form of expression of the convulsion varies according to its unconscious symbolic meaning. The most frequent form of the convulsion simply represents a repetition of those defence movements which the patient made when he was threatened with being shattered when he was buried. The convulsive attacks always take place when the ideas regarding those events are subconscious, and the strongly repressed affects which are bound to them, are associatively stimulated. A door slammed, a thunder-clap, a distant shot, makes the patient break down, and his previously unconscious anxiety idea becomes over-weighted. Terror and dread of death here generally form the primary basis for the dissociation of the psyche and for the attack-like mastery of the conscious by the unconscious.

A soldier who has once been paralysed for a time through the emotion of terror in his conscious ego is in many ways no longer in the position to satisfy consciously the repression which the pressure of discipline demands. It is almost always the anger towards his superiors which brings on further convulsive attacks. During hypnosis, which lifts the curtain of this originally hallucinated dream-action during the attack, we see again and again the patient struggling with his highest superiors. He strikes, bites, stabs and shoots them, treads them under foot with terrible oaths. He here lets free the fiercest instincts against persons who restrained his conscious ego.

It is quite explicable why these kinds of attacks before they come for treatment are often associated with mutism. The patient denies himself in a certain degree the faculty of speech, because he is afraid of speaking certain words that might bring misfortune upon him.

In one case I succeeded even without hypnosis in directly making use of the convulsive attacks of the patient for treatment. I was able to become *en rapport* with the patient in the attack so that he informed me about the events which he actually hallucinated during the single convulsive attack.

The sphere of the purely psychic war injuries without any physical signs which can be treated in this way is also great. I mentioned above a case of stupor. It is quite comprehensible that it is more particularly the mental inhibitory phenomena which are accessible to this treatment, because the cessation of mental processes is brought about through an accumulation of affect which entirely owes its origin to definite war occurrences. The psycho-catharsis as a foundation for a further analytic treatment here works wonders.

I will take this opportunity of mentioning that as regards the war neurotic an abreaction by means of words is mostly not sufficient in this compressed form of treatment. The soldier is under the suggestion of the deed "an eye for an eye, a tooth for a tooth". His overburdened subconscious now is freed by means of an acted abreaction. On account of this I have for a long time proceeded to construct an upholstered dummy against which the neurotic fighting in his primitive human instinct victoriously frees himself.

The neuroses of anxiety and terror, so far as they have become manifest through war experiences, can be treated successfully. Nevertheless, it is to be noted that also in the feeling of guilt of the war neurotic not only are real, specific and complex conditioned war atrocities the inner kernel, but that things experienced only in phantasy may be important.

One of the most frequent war psycho-neurotic symptoms represents what after all is comprehensible without anything further, loss of memory. It may extend over a limited period of the war or over the whole of it, or even into pre-war times. The whole memory is blotted out in order that definite things should not be brought to mind. When these have once become conscious by means of the dream or hypnosis, and are pondered over, the tendency of the unconscious is robbed of its objects and the memory is again automatically re-introduced.

The frequent loss of other intellectual capabilities likewise is mostly made good after sufficient discharge of affect. It is easy to understand that just those capabilities which represent the person's highest art of sublimation, like artistic ones, would particularly suffer through the war experiences. Thus, a not unknown painter when a recruit in the war lost his ability for colour perception. My suggestion during hypnosis that he should at night dream in a picture the subconscious circumstances of his illness and then sketch it next day he promptly carried out and therewith contributed to the removal of a symptom which meant so much to him.

Regarding the condition of excitement and frenzy which I have had ample opportunity of treating, I need say nothing further after what has been said concerning the convulsive attacks. They represent the positive side to the negative one of the convulsions. They are evoked by association and refer in the direction of their affects to definite persons or events that in a characteristic manner have more or less been forgotten by the patients. The nature of the associative production often enables one to recognise the typical neurotic displacement, a projection outwards. There are numerous patients of this kind who readily have an attack of rage at the sight of an officer's shoulder knot or a doctor's overall, because they once had had to repress their rage against a definite officer or doctor by whom they had psychically felt themselves ill-used. A word further concerning the psychic illness of the genuine pension neurosis. Here again the interpretation of dreams particularly during hypnosis enables us to decide whether we are dealing with a genuine war psycho-neurosis or the frequently falsely accused conscious "ideas of covetousness". I have found that the real pension neurosis represents a kind of inferiority neurosis. The patient values himself higher than he feels he is valued by his environment. He has generally, in his opinion, performed some special military achievement. He has counted on a distinction or at least a certain promotion which he does not attain. An illness or wound finally raises him above the general mass of the unknown, and now the pension is the substitute for the missing iron cross or the lance corporal's button with which the patient endeavours to prove his particular value in opposition to the state.

It can be understood that relapses occur in what is on the whole a comparatively hasty treatment. However, with the help of the pure analytic method described the character of the relapse can be established without difficulty. Frequently it is solely a question of the patients getting into the old surroundings through re-employment by the military to which they are not psychically equal, and from which they have escaped with the help of their neurosis, and now they in defence react with a relapse.

On the other hand, it can frequently be established that the treatment on account of its shortness has not removed all the unconscious material. I might mention as an example a soldier who had suffered from states of excitement and convulsive attacks. After two treatments the states of excitement disappeared and within four weeks the attacks had ceased. The patient had to be discharged in spite of the fact that he still seemed somewhat distressed. After a few months he came back into the hospital on account of a recurrence of the attacks. In the treatment carried out when he had first been admitted into the hospital only those things came to light which were connected with his being blown up. During hypnosis on his second admission the patient said that he still had the feeling as though "someone was behind him". This feeling of anxiety often increased so terribly that he would have a convulsive attack. In this attack he constantly saw a dead Russian in a white shirt who threateningly demanded back a gold ring which the patient had taken from the Russian after killing him. This occurrence the patient had completely forgotten, but after I had talked it over with him when he was awake he became changed, alert and keen to work, and was now permanently cured of his convulsions.

These theoretical points which I have supported by means of practical examples will suffice for a primary representation of the symptomatology of the war neuroses. It is impossible within the compass of this contribution, with the abundance of material at my disposal, to represent the numerous forms of the neuroses not mentioned here, and still further as regards their unconscious conditionality.

In conclusion I should like to give a short description of the neurosis of a young civil servant, which despite the brevity of the treatment revealed with classical clearness a modified picture of the nature of the neurotic predisposition and the actual outbreak of the illness.

This illness, when looked at from the outside, seemed to be a complete war neurosis without any kind of "civilian" origin. The patient had been for a long time in the field and constantly in the front line and had been exposed to extraordinary hardships. He had been wounded and only fell ill with his neurosis after being blown up twice. He had a severe impediment in his speech in consequence of an almost complete intention spasm of his lips, combined with states of excitement and rage, and attacks of loss of consciousness. The first conversation showed that all the physical disabilities signified nothing to the patient, on the contrary, he was completely broken down in mind and body through his struggles and friction with his superiors. In the first dream the patient received a letter, which to his unbounded rage his father had already opened, so that the red lining to the envelope hung in shreds. In the hypnosis the patient during the reading aloud of this dream underwent an extraordinary state of excitation, in which he re-experienced his last blowing up with unspeakable anxiety and terror. The red envelope lining was the torn out jaw bone of a dear friend and comrade who had been shattered beside him at that explosion. His relation to his father came out, with anger at the thought that he (the father) did not esteem all the great performances which he had accomplished in the field and communicated to him. The next dream after this hypnosis brought up a scene between the father and son. The father in the robe of the public prosecutor forbade his son, according to the law, to speak with some women imprisoned and kept in an underground dungeon. The son started up in anger and said that he had his own law book which lay by one of those women. He went to get it and wandered through underground passages. He found in several rooms earlier loved women, but not his law book. At last he came into the last room and on the threshold his mother met him in her nightdress.

I do not think I need to add many words to this audience to arrive at the interpretation. The patient fulfilled his "law" when he volunteered for the war, in order to put himself over his father through his manliness and obtain his mother. The symbol of the envelope, which, destined for the son, was unjustly opened by the father, is clear in its significance. It is peculiar and interesting how in this letter, which contained for the patient the secret of his life, is shown in combined representation the uninterrupted connection of the origin and outbreak of the neurosis—from the female genitals to the corpse of the shattered friend, to the memory of the last complete breakdown of the ego through the explosion.

I have come to the end of my remarks, and hope that I have proved that the combined psycho-analytical method gives us to-day a true medical treatment for war neurotics. Those doctors who have devised a system of tortures, such as hunger cures, dark rooms, prohibition of letters, painful electric currents, etc. in order to extort from the patients the abandonment of their neurotic symptoms, unconsciously recognise the Freudian theory by the inversion of its fundamental principles. They make a torture of the treatment in order to force the neurotic "to flee into health". The doctor schooled in psycho-analysis does not need to hound in the opposite direction his patients who have been driven into illness. He releases him from the fetters of his unconscious mind and thus is in the position to guide the neurotic into health and save him.

III.

WAR SHOCK AND FREUD'S THEORY OF THE NEUROSES[7]
BY DR. ERNEST JONES, LONDON.

A MATTER that used to hamper the opponents of psycho-analysis to some extent was that there was no alternative theory of the neuroses seriously tenable. It was clearly impossible to explain all neurotic manifestations by the catch-word use of the two terms "heredity" and "suggestion", for our conceptions of heredity, however important in this connection they may well become in the future when more is known of the subject, are at present too vague to explain any complex psychological phenomena, and the idea of suggestion merely introduces yet another problem without solving any of the old ones.

The experience of neurotic affections engendered by the war, however, has enabled the critics of psycho-analysis to put forward the view that the factors invoked by Freud in explanation of these affections need not be present, and therefore cannot be regarded as essential, in the way maintained by him, whereas, on the other hand, a different set of factors is undeniably present and operative; not only so, but these latter factors are held to be all-sufficing, so that it is not necessary to search for any others in the ætiology of the conditions in question. Some opponents of psycho-analysis, particularly those more concerned with combating an unwelcome theory than with ascertaining truth, have even maintained that the experience of the war has proved *all* Freud's views to be utterly untenable and false.

It would be easy to criticise the standpoint thus adopted, though that is in no sense my purpose here. Two points alone may be raised. If, as some writers assert, the strain of war conditions is in itself sufficient to account for the development of a psychoneurosis without the introduction of any other factor, then how is one to explain the actual incidence of war neuroses? Neurotic symptoms amounting to a definite clinico-pathological condition are by no means so common as is sometimes stated. I do not know of any statistics on the matter, but I should be surprised to hear that more than 2 per cent. of the Army serving in France are affected in this way. This consideration in itself shews that some other factors than war strain must be involved, factors relating to the previous disposition of the men affected, and the problem is to determine what these are. In the second place, as

<hr>

[7] Read before the Royal Society of Medicine, Section of Psychiatry, April 9, 1918. Published in the Proceedings, Vol. XI. Reprinted in "Papers on Psycho-Analysis": Jones, 2nd. Ed. 1918, Ch. XXXIII, p. 564. (Baillière, Tindall & Cox.).

to the dogmatic assertion that Freud's theory of the psychoneuroses cannot apply to those arising under war conditions. An essential feature of this theory is that psychoneuroses result from unconscious mental conflicts. To ascertain whether these are operative in a given case, therefore, it is obviously necessary to employ some method, such as psycho-analysis, which gives access to the unconscious. It may, I think, be taken as certain that those who deny the action of these conflicts in either the war neuroses or in what, by way of contradistinction, must be called the peace neuroses, have not thought it necessary to use any such method, and they thus place themselves in a position very similar to that of a writer who would on *a priori* grounds deny the details or even the existence of histology without ever having looked through a microscope, the only avenue to histology. I choose this simile because it seems to me that the relation of psycho-analysis to clinical psychiatry is not at all inaptly described[8] as being like that of histology to anatomy. Or one might draw an analogy from a strictly medical field. If some one were to take a series of cases of tuberculosis supervening on measles or typhoid, and then maintain that because this ætiological factor was present therefore no microorganism could be, so that Koch's views as to the causation of tuberculosis were entirely unfounded, one would surely have the right to ask whether any search for the bacillus had been made in the cases in question, and to satisfy oneself that the observer had grasped the difference between essential and merely exciting causes of disease. If the answer to both these inquiries were in the negative, I think it will be agreed that no great weight would be attached to the claim that Koch's theory of the nature of tuberculosis had been demolished. Yet this is precisely the order of scientific thinking evinced by those who maintain that Freud's theory of the neuroses has been demolished by the simple observation that they may manifest themselves under the stress of warfare.

I do not mean, however, to assert the contrary of this proposition—namely, that the validity of Freud's theory has been proved in the case of war neuroses, as I should maintain it has been in the case of peace neuroses. I simply hold that the matter is at present *sub judice*, and must remain so until sufficiently extensive investigations shall have settled the question one way or the other. It so happens that the traumatic neuroses are the field in psychopathology that has hitherto been the least explored by psycho-analysis even in peace time, while the opportunity of psycho-analytic investigation of the war neuroses has, in this country at least, been so meagre that the time is not ripe for any generalisation on the subject. Personally I have examined a considerable number of cases in the cursory way that is usual in hospital work, but I have been able to make an intensive study in only some half-dozen cases, and I do not know of any other cases that have been investigated by the psycho-analytic method. In spite of this paucity of material, a feature inherent in intensive work, the critic of psycho-analysis may legitimately demand of the analyst, who advances considerable pretensions in regard to understanding the pathology of neurotic affections in general, that he should be able to formulate some tentative conception of the relation between the phenomena commonly observed in the war neuroses and the psycho-analytical theory. In the following remarks an attempt will be made to meet this demand, although, as has just been

[8] By Freud, "Allgemeine Neurosenlehre", 1917, S. 286.

explained, there can be no question of solving the numerous and as yet unstudied problems raised by the observations made in connection with war shock.

It is desirable in the first place to clear away some general misconceptions on the subject. The task of assimilating our new experiences in connection with the war with any previously held theory of neurotic affections has undoubtedly been rendered more difficult by the attitude of those workers whose interest in such problems is of contemporary origin. They lay much too much emphasis on the newer and perhaps more sensational aspects of the phenomena observed, instead of trying to correlate the more familiar and better understood ones. This attitude has been so pronounced with some writers that one might almost imagine that before the war there had never been such calamities as wrecks, earthquakes, and railway accidents, and that men had never been tried to the limit of their endurance with privation, fatigue, and danger, while familiar symptoms like hysterical blindness and paralysis are thought worthy of detailed description and are treated almost as novelties in psychological medicine. So far as I know, however, although some symptoms—e.g., dread of shells—assume a form that is coloured by war experiences, no symptom, and hardly any grouping of symptoms, occurs in war neuroses that is not to be met with in the neuroses of peace, a fact which in itself would suggest that fundamentally very similar agents must be at work to produce the neurosis in both cases.

Another very prevalent misconception, one strengthened by the official use of that unfortunate catch-word "shell-shock", is that war neuroses constitute a more or less unitary syndrome. It is so often forgotten that the term "shell-shock" can only mean, and no doubt was originally intended to mean, a certain ætiological factor, and not the disease itself. I have preferred to use the less ambiguous and more obviously ætiological term "war-shock," one coined, I think, by Eder[9]. Even when the term "shell-shock" is avoided, its place is usually taken by the all-embracing expression "neurasthenia"—in most cases, in fact, where there are no physical symptoms of hysteria present. True neurasthenia in its strict sense, on the contrary, is a relatively rare complaint, certainly in anything like a pure form; I have not come across a single case myself in connection with the war. The results of war strain are anything but unitary; most of the diverse forms of neurosis and psychoneurosis are found to be represented, and until these are adequately distinguished one from another it is impossible to make any satisfactory study of their individual pathology. A further point still more often overlooked, and perhaps even more important, is that not only are the results diverse, but the ætiological factors concerned in war strain are much more complex than is sometimes realised. Careful study of the cases shews that what was the most important pathogenetic agent with one patient had nothing to do with the neurosis of a second patient, although he may have been equally exposed to its influence. For instance, the sight of a near friend being killed may have greatly affected one soldier and been closely related to his subsequent neurosis, whereas with a second patient who has gone through the same experience there may be no connection between it and *his* neurosis; the same applies to the other painful features of warfare, the

---

[9] Eder, "War Shock," 1917.

tension of waiting under shell fire, the experience of being buried alive, and so on. These considerations indicate the great importance of the individual factor predisposing to particular neurotic reactions, and point to the necessity for careful dissection of the various pathogenetic factors in a number of cases before making generalisations as to the way in which the numerous separate influences grouped together as war strain may operate.

Coming now to the points of contact between war experience and Freud's theory, one may remark, to begin with, how well the facts of the war itself accord with Freud's view of the human mind as containing beneath the surface a body of imperfectly controlled and explosive forces which in their nature conflict with the standards of civilisation. Indeed, one may say that war is an official abrogation of civilised standards. The manhood of a nation is in war not only allowed, but encouraged and ordered to indulge in behaviour of a kind that is throughout abhorrent to the civilised mind, to commit deeds and witness sights that are profoundly revolting to our æsthetic and moral disposition. All sorts of previously forbidden and buried impulses, cruel, sadistic, murderous and so on, are stirred to greater activity, and the old intrapsychical conflicts, which, according to Freud, are the essential cause of all neurotic disorders, and which had been dealt with before by means of "repression" of one side of the conflict, are now reinforced, and the person compelled to deal with them afresh under totally different circumstances.

It is plain, as MacCurdy has well pointed out[10], that men entering the Army, and particularly on approaching the battle-field, have to undergo a very considerable readjustment of their previous attitudes of mind and standards of conduct, a readjustment which is much greater in the case of some men than in that of others, and also one which some men find it much more easy to accomplish satisfactorily than do others. The man's previous standards of general morality, of cleanliness and æsthetic feeling, and of his relation to his fellow-man, have all to undergo a very considerable alteration. In all directions he has to do things that previously were repugnant to his strongest ideals. These ideals are ascribed by some—e.g., Trotter[11], and, following him, MacCurdy—to the operation of the herd instinct, in other words to the influence of the social *milieu* in which he may happen to have been brought up. I think personally that behind this influence there are still deeper factors at work of a more individual order, derived essentially from hereditary tendencies and the earliest relation of the child to its parents. However this may be, it is certain that every one has such ideals, though he may not describe them under this name, and that in the course of development he insensibly builds up a series of standards of which his ego approves—and which I therefore propose to refer to by Freud's term of the "ego ideal"—together with a contrasting series of which his ego disapproves.

As every student of genetic psychology knows, this gradual building up is never performed smoothly, but always after a number of both conscious and unconscious internal conflicts between the conscious ego on the one side and various impulses and desires on the other, after a series of partial renunciations and com-

---

[10] MacCurdy, "War Neuroses", *Psychiatric Bull.*, July, 1917, pp. 252, 253.
[11] Trotter, "Instincts of the Herd in Peace and War", 1916.

promises. Further, it is exceptional for the whole result to be satisfactory; there always remain certain fields—more especially in the realm of sex—where the resolution of the conflict is an imperfect one, and it is just from this imperfect resolution that, according to Freud, neurotic affections arise. The question whether a neurosis will result in a given case is essentially a quantitative one. The mind has the capacity of tolerating without harm a certain amount of stimulation from these internal impulses and desires that are not in unison with the ego, and when this limit is passed the energy derived from them flows over into neurotic manifestations. The mind has several methods for dealing with the energy of the anti-ego impulses successfully—that is to say, without the impairment of mental health— and it is only when these methods are inadequate to deal with the whole that neurosis ensues. Two of these methods may especially be noted. One is the deflection of the energy in question from its primitive and forbidden goal to another one in harmony with the more social standards of the ego; as every schoolmaster knows, sport is an excellent example of this. When the primitive goal was a sexual one, this process of deflection, here on to a non-sexual goal, has been given the name of "sublimation", but there are similar refining and modifying processes at work in connection with all anti-ego impulses—e.g., cruelty. A second method is to keep the energy in a state of repression in the unconscious, the conscious mind refusing to deal directly with it and guarding itself against its influence by erecting a dam or barrier against it, known as a reaction-formation. Thus in the case of primitive cruelty, a cruel child may develop into a person to whom the very idea of inflicting cruelty is alien and abhorrent, the original impulse having been quite split off from the ego into the unconscious, and its place taken in consciousness by the reaction-formation barrier of horror and sensitiveness to pain and suffering. In such ways as these a state of practical equilibrium is attained in the normal, the power of the ego-ideal having proved sufficient either to utilise for its own purposes (by means of modifying) or to keep at bay, the impulses and desires that are out of harmony with it. In some people the state of equilibrium thus attained is of considerable stability, they have what is popularly called a reserve of mental and moral force with which they can meet disappointments, difficulties, and emergencies of various kinds in life, which means in practice that their capacity for readjustment to radically new situations is fairly elastic.

Now, on approaching the field of war the readjustment necessary is one of the more difficult ones experienced in life, although it is by no means so difficult as can arise in various situations appertaining to the field of sex. It is an adjustment which practice shews is possible to the large majority of men, but there is no doubt that the success with which it is carried out is extremely variable in different people; and it probably varies in the same person from time to time for either internal reasons or for external reasons relating to the precise environment at the moment, to the precise war experiences through which they may be passing. It is further clear that the readjustment is likely to vary in its success almost entirely with the success with which the earlier adjustments were made during the development of the individual. This statement is meant to carry more than its obvious meaning that the more stable a man is the more surely can he meet the problems and difficulties of warfare; it has a deeper implication. Namely, there is an important relationship between the two phases of difficult adjustment, the current one and the older one. Fundamentally it is the same difficulty, the same conflict; it is only the form that is different. Let us suppose, for instance, that the original difficulty in adjustment was over the matter of cruelty, that in childhood the conflict between strong tendencies of this kind and perhaps specially strong ideals of the contrary sort was an exceptionally sharp one, so that it was never very satisfactorily resolved, though a working equilibrium may have been established on the basis of powerful reaction-formations and various protective devices for avoiding in every possible way contact with the subject of cruelty. Such a man may well have unusual difficulty in adapting himself to the cruel aspects of war, which really means that his long-buried and quite unconscious impulses to cruelty, impulses the very possibility of whose existence he would repudiate with horror, are stimulated afresh by the unavoidable sights and deeds of war. In bayonet practice, for instance, the man is taught how best to inflict horrible injuries, and he is encouraged to indulge in activities of this order from the very thought of which he has all his life been trying to escape. He now has to deal afresh with the old internal conflict between the two sides of his nature, with the added complication that there has to take place an extensive revaluation of his previous standards, and in important respects an actual reversal of them. He has to formulate new rules of conduct, to adopt new attitudes of mind, and to accustom himself to the idea that tendencies of which he had previously disapproved with the whole strength of his ego-ideal are now permissible and laudatory under certain conditions. One would get a very erroneous view of the picture I am trying to draw if one imagined that the process of readjustment in question goes on in the person's consciousness. This is never entirely true, and often not at all true; the most important part of the readjustment, and often the whole of it, is quite unconscious. We thus see that to obtain a proper understanding of the problems of an individual case, and to be able to deal with them practically in therapeutics, it is often necessary to appreciate the relation between a current conflict and an older one, for the real strength and importance of the current one is often due to the fact that it has aroused buried and imperfectly controlled older ones.

I have taken the one instance of cruelty, but there are many others in connection with warfare. It may, indeed, be said in general that the process of re-adaptation in regard to war consists of two distinct sides: on the one hand, war effects an extensive release of previously tabooed tendencies, a release shewn in endless ways—for instance, even in the language of camps; and on the other hand the acquiring of a strict discipline and self-control along lines widely different from those of peace-times. The one is a correlative of the other, and we have perhaps in these considerations a psychological explanation of the feature of military life that is so puzzling to most civilians—namely, the extraordinary punctiliousness that a rigid discipline attaches to matters which to the outsider appear so trivial. An indisciplined army has always been the bane of commanders, and perhaps the risks attaching to indiscipline are related to the release of imperfectly controlled impulses that war deliberately effects.

The way in which a relative failure in war adaptation may lead to a neurosis can be illustrated by a parallel drawn from the more familiar problems of peace neuroses. Imagine a young woman who has never been able to reconcile the sexual sides of her nature with her ego ideal, and whose only way of dealing with that aspect of life has been to keep it at as great a distance from her consciousness as possible. If now she gets married, it may happen that she will find it impossible to effect the necessary reconciliation, and that, being deprived of the *modus vivendi*—namely, the keeping sexuality at a distance—which previously made it possible to maintain a mental equilibrium, she develops a neurosis in which the repressed sexual desires achieve a symbolic and disguised expression. Similarly in a war neurosis when the old adjustment between the ego-ideal and the repressed impulses is taken away, it may prove impossible to establish a fresh one on the new conditions, and then the repressed impulses will find expression in some form of neurotic symptom.

So far as I can judge, the specific problems characteristic of the war neuroses are to be found in connection with two broad groups of mental processes. One of these relates to the question of war adapttation considered above, the other to that of fear. The latter is hardly to be regarded as a sub-group of the former, inasmuch as there is no readjustment or transvaluation of values concerned, as there typically is with the former. The moral attitude towards fear, and the conflicts arising in connection with it, remain the same in war as in peace. In both cases it is considered a moral weakness to display or be influenced by fear, and especially to give in to it at the cost of not doing one's duty. The soldier who would like to escape from shell fire is, so far as moral values are concerned, in the same position as a man in peace-time who will not venture his life to save a drowning child. Indeed, the conflict cannot be as sharp in the case of the soldier, for he would find very widespread and thorough sympathy for his quite comprehensible desire, and there would be much less social blame or guilt attaching to him than to the man in the other situation mentioned. So that the problem of fear, which we all agree plays a central part in connection with the typical war neuroses, seems to be apart from that of war adaptation in general as expounded above.

Before discussing the problem of fear, however, I should like at this point to review the position and see how far we have got in the attempt to approximate the facts of war neuroses to the psycho-analytical theory. This theory of the neuroses is a very elaborate one, including many problems of unconscious mechanisms, distinctions between the predispositions and mechanisms characteristic of the different neuroses, and so on, but it is possible to formulate the main principles of it along fairly simple lines, and I now propose to do this in a series of statements.

(1) The first principle in Freud's theory of neurotic symptoms is that they are of volitional origin. This principle, long suspected by both the medical and the lay public, and the real reason why in the past they have been so confounded with malingering, would be at once evident were it not for the fact that it is not true of volition in the ordinary sense of conscious deliberate voluntary purpose. In other words, it is not true of the will as a whole, but only of a part of it—namely, a part that the patient is not aware of. Thus, neuroses are not diseases or accidents that happen to a person, as the French school of psychopathology maintains, but are

phenomena produced and brought about by some tendency in the person's mind, and for specific purposes. Freud distinguishes three classes of motives that operate in this way, one essential, the other two not. The indispensable one is an unconscious desire to obtain pleasure by gratifying in the imagination some repressed and dissociated impulse, a motive, therefore, arising in the part of the mind that is not in harmony with the ego-ideal. A second motive is to achieve some end in the outer world; for instance sympathy from an unkind husband, which the person finds easier to do by means of a neurosis than in other ways. The third set of motives has the same purpose as the last, but may be distinguished from it in that they concern the making use of an already existing neurosis rather than the helping to bring one about. Both the latter sets are usually, but not always, unconscious: more strictly, they are preconscious—that is, they do not relate to deeply buried tendencies, and so are correspondingly easy to reveal; Freud terms them the primary and secondary "gain of illness" respectively. Now I take it that this principle of volitional origin is no longer very widely questioned by modern psychopathologists, and in the case of war neuroses the main motives are visible and comprehensible enough—namely, the desire to find some good reason for escaping from the horrors of warfare.

(2) The second principle is that all neurotic symptoms are the product of an intrapsychical conflict which the person has failed satisfactorily to resolve, and that they constitute a compromise formation between the two conflicting forces. Here, again, I think that those who have been investigating the psychology of war neuroses will agree with this principle. MacCurdy,[12] in particular, has described in great detail the conflict that arises in soldiers between, on the one hand, the motives actuating to continuance at duty and concealment of growing sense of incapacity and apprehension, and, on the other, the awful sense of failure accompanying the sometimes almost overwhelming desire to escape from the horrors of their position. The neurosis offers a way out of this dilemma, the only way that the particular person is able to find, and the actual symptoms, which are often grossly incapacitating, such as blindness, represent the fulfilment of the desire against which the man has been fighting. We reach, therefore, the wish-fulfilment part of Freud's theory.

(3) The third principle is that the operative wish that leads to the creation of the neurosis is an unconscious one. Freud means this in the full sense of the word, and in this sense the principle has not yet been confirmed from the experience of the war neuroses. There are, however, different degrees of unconsciousness of a mental process, and the important point to Freud is not so much the degree of the unawareness in itself—this being largely an index of the repression—as the repression or dissociation that has led to the unawareness. What he maintains is that the wish producing the neurosis is one that is not in harmony with the ego-ideal, and which is therefore kept at as great a distance as possible from it. Anyone who has read the touching accounts given by MacCurdy or Rivers[13] of the shame that soldiers feel at their increasing sense of fear, and the efforts they make to fight

[12] MacCurdy, *op. cit.*

[13] Rivers, "The Repression of War Experience", *Proceedings of the Royal Society of Medicine*, 1918, xi (Sect. of Psych.), p. 1, Dec. 4, 1917.

against it, to conceal it from others, and if possible from themselves, will recognise that the wish in question is one alien to the ego-ideal and is well on in the first stages of repression, even if it is half-avowed.

(4) The fourth principle is that current repressed wishes cannot directly produce a neurosis, but do so only by reviving and reinforcing the wishes that have been repressed in older unresolved conflicts. According to Freud, a pathogenetic disappointment or difficulty in readjustment leads first to an introversion or turning inwards of feeling, and the wish that has been baulked seeks some other mode of gratification. It tends to regress back to an older period of life, and thus to become associated with similarly baulked and repressed wishes belonging to older conflicts. It is the combination of these two, the present and the old, that is the characteristic mark of the pathogenesis of neurotic disorders as distinct from other modes of reaction to the difficulties of life.

Freud considers that there are probably always three factors in the causation of any neurosis: a specific hereditary predisposition, secondly an unresolved infantile conflict which means that the person has not satisfactorily developed past a given stage of individual evolution—in other words, that he has been subjected to what is called an "infantile fixation" at a given point in development, and thirdly the current difficulty. There is a reciprocal relationship between these three factors, so that if any one is especially pronounced the others may be correspondingly less important. For instance, if the hereditary factor is very pronounced then a person may become neurotic from the quite ordinary experiences of childhood and adult life, for he is incapable of dealing adequately with them. In the case of war neuroses it is evident that the current factor is of the greatest importance, being, indeed, the only one that so far has attracted attention. The only traces of infantile factors I have seen noted have been the instances where the localisation of hysterical symptoms seems to have been determined in part by the site of old injuries, and in a general way the many traits of childhood, such as sensitiveness to slights, self-centredment, and desire to be guarded, protected, and helped, which are sometimes very evident in the cases of war neurosis.

We thus see that only one half of the psycho-analytical theory has so far been confirmed by the observations of war neuroses. According to this theory, there are typically two sets of wishes concerned in the production of any neurosis. One of these, the "primary gain of illness", a current one, alien to the conscious ego ideal, and therefore half repressed and only half conscious—if that—has not only been demonstrated by a number of observers, but has been shewn to be of tremendous importance, and certainly the effects of treatment largely turn on the way in which it is dealt with. The other factor, the infantile and altogether repressed and unconscious one, which, according to psycho-analysis, is also essential to the production of a neurosis, has not been systematically sought for, though I have found it in the few cases of which I have been able to make a full study. Its presence or absence is a matter of greater theoretical importance than might perhaps appear, even though its practical importance may often not be great. For my own part I have the utmost difficulty in believing that a current wish, however strong that is half conscious and sometimes fully conscious can ever in itself produce a neurosis, for it contradicts all one's knowledge concerning the nature of neuroses, as well as my experience, such as it is, of war neuroses themselves. I would therefore urge that no conclusion is possible on the matter one way or the other until adequate investigations have been carried out. That it has its practical side also will be pointed out when we come to consider the chronic cases where war neuroses pass over into peace ones.

(5) The principle of the psycho-analytical theory that has aroused the strongest opposition is that the primary repressed wish ultimately responsible for the neurosis is always of a sexual nature, so that the conflict is between the two groups of instincts that go to make up the whole personality, those concerned respectively with preservation of the self and of the species. Dr. MacCurdy has suggested to me that this is so only because, apart from war, there is no instinct that comes into such strong conflict with the ego-ideal as does the sexual one, but that in war the conflict between the instinct for self-preservation and the ego-ideal is enough to lead to a neurosis. This may seem very plausible, but I shall be surprised if it is confirmed by future research. That a neurosis, which after all is a disorder of the unconscious imagination, should arise from a conflict between two states of mind that are fully in contact with reality would be something entirely contradictory of our past experience, as would also a neurosis arising from a conflict between two tendencies both belonging to the ego. I shall venture to put forward an alternative hypothesis presently when discussing the subject of fear, which we have next to consider.

Freud states[14] that from one point of view all psychoneurotic symptoms may be regarded as having been constructed in order to prevent the development of fear — another point of contact between his theory and the observers of war neuroses, who would surely agree that fear is the central problem they have to deal with. By fear is here meant rather the mental state of dread and apprehension, increasing even into terror, and accompanied by well-marked bodily manifestations, a state for which psychopathologists have agreed to use the term "morbid anxiety" (or, shortly, "anxiety") in a special technical sense as being the nearest equivalent of the German word *Angst*.

Morbid anxiety is certainly the commonest neurotic symptom, and the theory of its pathogenesis has been the occasion of a very great deal of investigation,[15] with, in my opinion, very fruitful results. We meet it in the form of a general apprehensiveness of impending danger and evil, as the anxiety-neurosis, and also in hysteria in the form both of apparently causeless attacks of dread and of innumerable specific phobias. In all its forms its most striking feature is the disproportion between its intensity and its apparent justification, so that it seems at first sight extremely difficult to correlate with the biological view of fear as a useful instinct that guards against danger. Practically all modern investigations into its pathogenesis agree that it stands in the closest relation with unsatisfied and repressed

[14] Freud, *op. cit.*, S. 470.

[15] The latest discussion of the subject will be found in Freud's "Allgemeine Neurosenlehre," 1917, chapter xxv, "Die Angst". See also his papers in "Sammlung kleiner Schriften zur Neurosenlehre," 1906, chapters v, vi, vii, and a general review of the subject in my "Papers on Psycho-Analysis," 2nd ed., 1918, chapter xxvii, "The Pathology of Morbid Anxiety".

sexuality, and, in my judgment, the conclusion that morbid anxiety represents the discharge of repressed and unconscious sexual hunger is one of the most securely established in the whole of psychopathology; it is impossible here to consider the extensive evidence in support of this conclusion, and I can only refer to the published work on the subject[16].

The next question is: What is the relation between morbid anxiety as seen in peace neuroses and real—*i.e.*, objectively justified—fear, as seen in various situations of acute danger and so prominently in the war neuroses? The point of connection is the defensive character of the reaction. Morbid anxiety, as we are familiar with it in the peace neuroses, is a defensive reaction of the ego against the claims of unrecognised "sexual hunger" (*Libido*), which it projects on to the outside world—e.g., in the form of phobias—and treats as if it were an external object; it is, in a word, the ego's fear of the unconscious. But there appears to be an important difference between it and "real" dread in that the latter concerns only the ego itself, arises only in connection with external danger to the ego, and has nothing to do with the desires of repressed sexual hunger. One is tempted to say that the latter (real dread) is a normal protective mechanism that has nothing to do with the abnormal mechanism of morbid anxiety. Here, however, as elsewhere, the line between normality and abnormality is not so absolute as might appear, and consideration of the matter leads one to examine more closely into the nature of real dread itself. We then see that this can be dissected into three components, and that the whole reaction is not appropriate and useful as is commonly assumed. The reaction to external danger consists normally of a mental state of fear, which will be examined further in a moment, and in various activities suited to the occasion—flight, concealment, defence by fighting, or even sometimes by attacking. On the affective side there is, to begin with, a state of anxious preparedness and watchfulness, with its sensorial attentiveness and its motor tension. This is clearly a useful mental state, but it often goes on further into a condition of developed dread or terror which is certainly the very reverse of useful, for it not only paralyses whatever action may be suitable, but even inhibits the functioning of the mind, so that the person cannot judge or decide what he ought best to do were he able to do it. The whole reaction of "real" fear is thus seen to consist of two useful components and one useless one, and it is just this useless one that most resembles in all its phenomena the condition of morbid anxiety. Further, there is seen to be a complete lack of relation between development of dread and the degree or imminence of danger, nor does it bear any relation to the useful defensive activities. Thus, one does not flee because one is frightened, but because one perceives danger; in situations of extreme danger men very often respond with suitable measures of flight, fight, or what not, when they are not in the least degree frightened; on the other hand, the neurotic can be extremely frightened when there is no external danger whatever. The inference from these considerations is that even in situations of real danger a state of developed dread is not part of the useful biological mechanism of defence, but is an abnormal response akin to the neurotic symptom of morbid anxiety.

---

[16] *See* also Stekel, "Angstzustände," 2e. Aufl., 1912.

In a recent publication[17] Freud has made the striking suggestion that the developed dread sometimes found in situations of real danger is derived, not from the repressed sexual hunger that is directed towards external objects, as is the case with morbid anxiety of the peace neuroses, but from the narcissistic part of the sexual hunger that is attached to the ego, and I venture to suggest that we may here have the key to the states of terror with which we are so familiar in the war neuroses. The psycho-analytic investigations of recent years have laid increasing stress on the distinction between "object-libido", the sexual impulses that are directed outwards, and the "ego-libido", the narcissistic portion that is directed inwards and constitutes self-love. There is good reason to suppose that the latter is the more primary of the two, and also the more extensive—though the least explored as yet—so that it constitutes, as it were, a well from which externally directed sexuality is but on overflow. The analogy naturally occurs to one of the protoplasmic outpourings in the pseudopodia of the amœba, and the reciprocal relation of these to the main body seems to be similar to that between love of others and self-love. It has been known for some time that there is a limit on the part of the organism to tolerate without suffering more than a given quantity of sexual hunger in its familiar sense of impulses directed outwards, and analytic study of the psychoses, notably of paraphrenia, has shewn that the same is even more profoundly true of the narcissistic sexual hunger. In both cases, before other symptoms are formed so as to deal with the energies in question and bind them, the first thing that happens is a discharge in the form of morbid anxiety, so that we reach the comforting conclusion that a normal man would be entirely free from dread in the presence of any danger, however imminent, that he would be as fearless as Siegfried; it is a gratifying thought that there seem to be many such in our Army to-day. It seems to me probable that the intolerance of narcissistic sexual hunger which leads to dread in the presence of real danger is to be correlated with the inhibition of the other manifestations of the fear instinct, with the accumulated tension characteristic of the mode of life in the trenches.

I would suggest, therefore, that investigations be undertaken from this point of view with cases of war neurosis, especially the anxiety cases. Many of the features noted by MacCurdy[18], for instance, accord well with the picture of wounded self-love: thus, the lack of sociability, the sexual impotence and lack of affection for relatives and friends, the feeling that their personality has been neglected, or slighted, that their importance is not sufficiently recognised, and so on. Perhaps a new light may also be thrown in this way on the attitude of such patients towards death. I understand that a great part of the war neurotic symptoms, and the battle dreams in particular, have been widely interpreted as symbolising the desire to die so as to escape from the horrors of life, an interpretation that does not accord well with the equally widespread view that the fundamental cause of such neuroses is a fear of death. I greatly doubt, on the contrary, whether the fundamental attitude is either a fear of death in the literal sense or a desire for death. The conscious mind has difficulty enough in encompassing in the imagination the conception of absolute annihilation, and there is every reason to think that the unconscious mind is

[17] Freud, *op. cit.*, S. 502.
[18] MacCurdy, *op. cit.*, pp. 269-272.

totally incapable of such an idea. When the idea of death reaches the unconscious mind it is at once interpreted in one of two ways: either as a reduction of essential vital activity, of which castration is a typical form, or as a state of nirvana in which the ego survives, but freed from the disturbances of the outer world.

A word in conclusion as to the therapeutic aspects of psycho-analysis in the war neuroses. Even if it were possible, I see no reason whatever why a psycho-analysis should be undertaken in the majority of the cases, for they can be cured in much shorter ways. But I consider that a training in psycho-analysis is of the very highest value in treating such cases, from the understanding it gives of such matters as the symbolism of symptoms, the mechanisms of internal conflict, the nature of the forces at work, and so on, and there is certainly a considerable class of cases where psycho-analysis holds out the best, and sometimes the only, prospect of relief—namely, in those chronic cases where the war neurosis proper has, by association of current with older conflicts, passed over into a peace neurosis and become consolidated as such.

Lector House believes that a society develops through a two-fold approach of continuous learning and adaptation, which is derived from the study of classic literary works spread across the historic timeline of literature records. Therefore, we aim at reviving, repairing and redeveloping all those inaccessible or damaged but historically as well as culturally important literature across subjects so that the future generations may have an opportunity to study and learn from past works to embark upon a journey of creating a better future.

This book is a result of an effort made by Lector House towards making a contribution to the preservation and repair of original ancient works which might hold historical significance to the approach of continuous learning across subjects.

HAPPY READING & LEARNING!

LECTOR HOUSE
LECTOR HOUSE LLP
E-MAIL: lectorpublishing@gmail.com

www.ingramcontent.com/pod-product-compliance
Lightning Source LLC
LaVergne TN
LVHW090218180726
843492LV00012B/1109